About The Author

 Erin Parker is an economics student at Stanford University. She has had three investment banking internships spanning UBS (private wealth management), FT Partners (financial technology coverage), and J.P. Morgan in New York (syndicated and leveraged finance).

She is co-president of Blyth Fund, a six-figure student investing group and is on the board of Stanford's premier finance organization, Stanford Finance. Erin is also the Finance Director of Gumball Capital, a student-run startup whose mission is poverty alleviation.

She was a panelist at the Stanford Women in Business "I Don't Know to CEO" conference and a speaker at the Raza Day Event on "Make It Happen Ability: The Secret to Success".

In her spare time, Erin is either training for a marathon, espresso-bar hopping, or voraciously reading a pile of books at the bookstore.

Banking Life

"Make it a point to walk around the floor and socialize at
least once if not multiple times a day."

How To Be A Boss: 3 Rules For Woman In Banking

Rule #1: Bosses don't slave away at their desk all day. When the right time comes, they're out with people who make it happen, drinking martinis and talking business.

Problem: hard work ethic and an impressive work product are only a mere part of the success formula in business. Women in banking who are always and forever cranking miss out on opportunities that arise from socializing with co-workers.

Solution: don't aim for *hard work*: aim for **visibility**. You already work hard, but you need to strive to be visible.

1. Make it a point to walk around the floor and s̲ocialize at least once if not multiple times a day.
2. Don't sign up for or create work for work's sake– making buddies in the office in your spare time is much more important.
3. Practice an unusually strong handshake and a super-confident "Good morning!" An unusually **strong handshake** is a solid way to leave your mark and a good thing to be remembered for.
4. Don't just make friends– make **buddies**.

Rule #2: Dress like a boss.

Problem: Many women dress to look pretty. By dressing to look pretty you're dressing to make yourself attractive to guys. In the office, your goal isn't to look attractive, your goal is to be respected. Attractiveness is required, too, but it's secondary.

Solution: When going to work, women in banking should aim to **dress like a boss**. Dress like you earn $10 million a year. Dress like you just ran a $20 billion deal. Dress like you're in charge of the entire financial restructuring division.

1. Stick with a **full suit** – pants suit or A-line knee length skirt suit. It's most professional and formal to wear a collared shirt or a really nice blouse underneath.
2. When you look at yourself in the mirror, ask yourself, do I look like a boss?
3. Carry a **blazer** with you everywhere; it screams power and credibility. Nothing goes better with women in banking than blazers. If you don't want to wear a blazer, a collared shirt is your next best bet.

Rule #3: Socialize with the guys.

Problem: It's good for women in banking to have support from your fellow females but if you're getting breakfast then coffee then lunch and dinner with just your girl mates, you're severely limiting your visibility. I'm not saying you have to go out, bar hop, and play beer games with the dudes every weekend, but there's one thing I noticed guys develop at the work place that women in banking need to develop too– *buddies*.

Solution: Get **buddies**. Develop camaraderie. How do you build camaraderie? **Go out! Do stuff together, bond**.

Here's what guys do. They drop by each other's desks Friday afternoon, punch each other on the shoulder and invite each other out for a cold beer. They all go together drinking and talk at various bars. Usually out of drunken fun, some adventure transpires. The next day at work those same guys are like, "Hey man last night was so money!" and going forward they act like best friends forever.

On the other side of the desk sits Miss Goody Two Shoes overhearing the conversation working on a pile of stuff and not having fun. **Don't be Miss Goody Two Shoes!**

Here's how to buddy up:

1. Take the **initiative** and personally invite people to go out
2. Go **bar hopping** and have fun– talk, play games, relax– oh, and buy your own drinks
3. The next day, go up to your buddies and **reminisce** loudly about all the fun you had
4. If you're extra cool, invent a special handshake or a **nickname**

This is the 80% of business that completes the 20% of hard work that gets done in the office. **Be part of it. Be a boss.**

Client Outreach Tip: Take Calls

I did one simple thing that helped me impress my superiors and mature as an analyst: **I took client calls.**

A lot of interns are afraid to speak with clients. They're afraid that they'll say something stupid, make the bank look stupid, and ruin their reputations as finance workers. This mindset of fear and uncertainty will not take you where you want to go in life. If you're going to work in finance, you have to learn confidence.

By taking client calls whenever I could, I was able to save the VP time by taking on those basic tasks myself. Also, by actively working with clients, **I was able to learn my trade much faster and assimilate into my role as an analyst.**

Taking on an active role with clients is simple but requires initiative. I'd answer phones when they rang and would include my phone number at the bottom of emails to offer my help. **Whenever someone would CC me on a deal, I would respond politely to the client and tell them they should feel free to reach me at my number any time they had questions.**

Simple actions like those got me a lot of calls, which is great because I got a lot of practice and slowly had more time to make deals. **Clients generally asked ask the same types of questions over and over, so I became faster at answering them as time went on.** They wanted to know basic things like what fees they were being charged, what percentage of the deal they had to put in money for, and so on.

Just through simple actions like being available for phone calls, you can set yourself apart and sharpen your skills as an analyst.

4 Tips To Ace Your Assignments And Impress Your Superiors

In addition to your basic investment banking internship preparation, you'll need to start looking for the competitive edge that will put yourself on the radars of your superiors.

When you're first starting out with your internship, the best way to set yourself apart from the other interns is to **ace all of the small assignments and projects they give you.**

4 Tips To Ace Your Assignments:

1. **Go above and beyond.** Your superiors will often ask you for random things like a record of the prime rate from 1990 to the current day. For a task like that, you should pull the data actually starting with 1988, make your chart, and print it out. Make your chart actually shows the prime rate. You don't want people to think you don't even know what the prime rate is.
2. **Check for mistakes.** If you do see a mistake in your work, you should go back and print it out again and again until it's perfect.
3. **Work carefully.** There are some interns who will throw something together and then send it out in an email without checking it. Carelessness like that can really came back and bite them in the butt because the VP will conclude that they can't even rely on them to pull simple data. In situations where they give you seemingly simple tasks like pulling data, spend extra time to make sure that you've pulled the correct data. If you can't even pull data flawlessly, they won't **trust** you with something that will be sent to a client.
4. **Double check your work.** The best way to pull data flawlessly is to print it out and check it with a pen. Line by line. Look at every data point and use a pen to put a check mark next to every data point you verify. Only once the entire data page is filled with those check marks should you print and send it out.

You can't just dress like an experienced banker and expect people to take you seriously. You also need to play the part and play it well.

3 Steps To Win Deal Flow

Your primary goal should be **deal flow.** Get staffed on live deals and keep them coming your way.

There are 3 steps to winning deal flow:

Step 1: Ace all the small projects and assignments that are given to you.

Take them seriously, do them well, and even **go above and beyond** if you're hungry for more (which you should be). Analysts and senior bankers use these small projects to test your mettle, so doing well on the smaller stuff means deal flow in the near future.

Step 2: Introduce yourself to everyone on the floor and ask for deals.

Yes. Make the ask. But (for obvious reasons) don't say, "Can you give me something to do?" Don't say, "Do you have anything for me to work on?" Instead phrase it as, "Can I help you with anything?" Bankers like to hear the phrase **high bandwidth** so you can try and sound more banker-ish and say, "Would you like some help? I've got high bandwidth right now!"

On days when you don't have anything to do, **work the floor** by going around to everyone, asking them how they're doing and offering to help. Later on, try sending short, one-sentence emails. Try changing the time you make your ask. At some places, deal flow regularly didn't come around until 10pm. I'd ask at 10pm, get assigned some slides, and do them first thing in the morning! Make the ask.

Step 3: Think big picture and show off.

If you really want to learn banking and not just do banking, try to understand how what you just worked on contributed to the bigger part of the deal. Ask yourself, "Why is this important? Who is going to see this?"

It's good to develop the habit of **getting context** by reading up on the company. Read your company's 10K, 10Q, Analyst Reports, and Rating Agency Reports. Also **read the legal documents** behind your deal (term sheets, credit agreements) because as a VP you'll be negotiating the terms behind these documents and the sooner you can garner an understanding of the weeds in the **deal process**, the better.

Then, take what you read and show off. Get brownie points. Instead of asking, "So what are the next steps?" go beyond and ask about how the client felt, for example ,"How did the meeting go? Did the client respond well to our pitch?" Or, "Did the deck read well when you presented it to the client? Anything I could improve for next time?"

If you're going for super-ninja status, start thinking about ways you can improve your product. For example, "I noticed that last time we met the client, we talked about XYZ but didn't include it in our model, maybe we could add XYZ column to illustrate our pricing more effectively." Or even, "I noticed we usually sort the comps by company size...maybe we could sort by ratings and then by company size so that our clients can see the landscape of competitors more intuitively?"

It's not about asking questions to try and sound smart, it's about getting into the weeds and **asking questions to calibrate a finer understanding** of what goes on. Your ability to receive deal flow improves the more you take care of your deals. When in doubt, ask yourself, "If I was the client and I was analyzing this to assist my business, what would I like to see?"

Put yourself in the client's shoes when looking at your powerpoints, models, and ask yourself, "Do I understand this? Do I like this? Can it be better?" I also liked to ask myself, "If I was VP today, would I know what to do with this?" I've found these are both solid strategies for **understanding the bigger picture**.

Serious Suit Shopping Tricks For Women In Business

Here is a wonderful guest article by my good friend Alice Nam, a senior at Stanford and Co-President of the Stanford 85Broads women in business group. She's a real fashionista, a fantastic writer, and will be working with McKinsey when she graduates. I hope you enjoy this article as much as I did – her advice is very applicable to every aspiring business woman! Cheers!

For some of us, between the empty coffee cups and abandoned problem sets that marked the recruiting process, there was one thing to look forward to: shopping.

Alas, as you wandered through Nordstrom with wide eyes and a $300 check from your mother, you realized two things– (1) most suits fit like they were made for your mother and (2) there is pretty much only one high-end brand that doesn't make you look like your frumpy middle school principal. Unfortunately, $300 will only get you ¾ of a Theory suit.

No worries! The goal of this guide is to help you find that perfect suit without taking out more student loans.

Before you get started, there are 2 things I wish someone had told me:

1. Start early.

I felt really dumb buying a suit before I got any interviews, so I didn't. When I did get an interview, I wasted a day at the mall in tears trying to find a suit (I'm a 00 Petite). In the end, I was stressed because I didn't like the suit, and I didn't know how I was going to pay off my credit card at the end of the month. Have faith in yourself. You WILL have an interview at some point in your life, and **you WILL need a suit**– so start looking now. Trust me, you'll look better the day of your interview and you'll save a lot of money.

2. Accept the challenge.

Most girls who like fashion express themselves through their wardrobe. Once you get that offer, feel free to wear what you please, but until then, your quest is to find that classic black (or dark grey) suit– **it's like the "little black dress" of interviews**. No provocative Helmut Lang blazers with striped arms, or zippers or whatever. The point is to find a boring suit that makes YOU look great. It's a challenge, especially in the staid world of womens' suits. So let's get started.

There are, in my mind, 2 steps to suit shopping.

Look everywhere for that dream suit – thrift stores, your mother's closet (if she lets you), Saks Fifth Avenue– everywhere. Don't get snobby and diss Brooks Brothers because you think that's where old ladies from Connecticut shop. Stores like Banana Republic and Ann Taylor have been in the suit making business for a long time, and each year they have more and more styles for their biggest, growing demographic: young women. On the other hand, don't shy away from walking into a Hugo Boss boutique. You won't be able to afford so much as a handkerchief, but you'll get an idea of what works for your body.

In other words, **try on everything**. As always, you should shop with a friend who isn't afraid to say what she thinks, but if that's not possible, bring a camera. A representative at Neiman Marcus actually recommended this and took a picture with my phone. That way, you can compare different fits in the comfort of your dorm room and get other people's opinions.

Oh, and make friends with the representatives at all these stores; some of them have been fitting suits longer than you've been alive. If they really like you, they just might tell you when everything is going to go on sale.

Okay, now suppose you've found a suit you love and surprise (!) it's from Theory and there's just no way you can afford it at sticker price.

Now we're onto **the second part of suit shopping: how to afford the damn thing.** I've listed some tried-and-tested strategies below:

Outlets

Outlets are probably a few hours away from where you live, but you're about to save a few hundred bucks, it's worth your time and the gas miles. Even if you're the heiress to an oil company and don't have to worry about the price of your suit, you should still go to outlets because they have styles from previous years. Go often; these places are always getting new shipments from stores that are trying to get rid of their inventory. If you live near Stanford, the Great America outlet is about 20 minutes away and features Off Saks and a Banana Republic among others.

Shopstyle and Shop It To Me

These two web start-ups are staples for serious shoppers. On Shopstyle, you can search for a suit and compare prices and sizes on different websites. Remember, at a lot of stores (Nordstrom for sure), there is some sort of price matching policy, so if you find the suit you want at Bergdorf Goodman but Saks has your size, be bold and ask a sales representative if you can get it at the cheaper price. The worst they can say is no.

Shop It To Me is more hands-off: you enter the brand you want to track and the size, and they e-mail you when there are items on sale. On average, you'll get up to 30% off using this method, which isn't as great as the 50%+ you'd save at an outlet. If you want to make it more worth your time, sign up for e-mails from these stores (route them to a different folder or e-mail address so they don't clutter your inbox).

After everything goes on sale, Neiman Marcus will ALWAYS have a promotion in a few weeks where you get at least an addition 25% off if you buy something on sale, and you'll only find out about it if you check their site every day or sign up for their spam.

Credit Card– ONLY IF YOU CAN PAY IT OFF

I'm kind of scared to recommend this, but you're about to apply to be a banker, so you might as well learn to manage your own finances. In addition to rewards, some stores offer special☐ discounts to cardholders. Every other week, I get an email with a 30% coupon for Banana Republic if I use their card. I'm sure other stores have a similar policy, so do some sleuthing.

Now suppose, you're like me, and you didn't take any of my advice. It's ok. Remember– they're not hiring your suit. They're hiring you.

I live in the Cowell Cluster at Stanford with all the sororities, and at some level, it's impossible to ignore the drama of **what to wear** when you're surrounded by trendy girls. It's also psychological; there is so much at stake in the recruiting process, so there's a tendency to micromanage the things you can control. But no matter what you end up wearing the day of your interview, walk out the door, and never think about your suit again.

Just as a final anecdote, the day of my final rounds with McKinsey (not banking, I know, but☐ bear with me) I spilled Red Bull on myself as I was leaving my hotel room. I had a heart attack for 10 seconds. Then I changed into a wrinkled black dress I'd had no intention of wearing, threw on the same blazer I'd worn the day before at first rounds, and marched out the door.☐

I got the offer, and I forgot about that whole crisis until I was writing this article. In the end, it's just a suit. Now go network or something.

- Alice Nam

6 Simple Tips For Affordable Women's Suit Shopping

I decided to write an article on affordable suit shopping because I realized many guides in magazines were just ridiculous– featuring "affordable" $3000 suits– yeah right. Although you're supposed to *invest* in a good suit for interviews you shouldn't have to go bankrupt.

Things To Keep In Mind While Shopping:

1. Choose your heels first and then tailor your pants to your heel.
2. Best heel length is 2-3 inches.
3. Your pants need to be fitted, but you shouldn't be able to see the hills of your butt or the contours of your inner thighs.
4. Invest in a good suit jacket for the ultimate "power look" (my personal favorite is from Anne Taylor).
5. Buy a pair of flats (I get mine at Payless) to wear while you're walking around or near work–they'll fit in your bag and aren't bulky like sneakers.

Budget #1: Ultra Low

Strategy 1: Get a suit from a relative and have it tailored. In high school I had a size 11 suit jacket made in the 1980s tailored to a size 3 for $20. I still have it and I still wear it.

Strategy 2: Go suit shopping at thrift stores like Goodwill and Salvation Army. Target thrift stores near high net worth cities for better selection. The Goodwill in Palo Alto, California regularly has some ridiculously good brands and selection. I've gotten some solid brand name sweaters from there for around $10 a piece.

Budget #2: Medium

Strategy 1: Scour the aisles of Ross and Burlington. They often have nice looking suit sets on display, but if they're currently not in season, focus on finding good blouses and skirts.

Strategy 2: Shop at the JC Penney suit department. They sell full suits that cost $100, but budget in $20-$30 for tailoring. I used to get my suits at JC Penney.

Budget #3: High

Strategy 1: My personal favorite stores are now Banana Republic and Ann Taylor from which I buy pants at around $60 and suit jackets at around $100-$200. I shop shortly after New Years to take advantage of the clearance sales.

Strategy 2: I think the best fitted, collared, suit shirts are at H&M for around $20. They come in every color from standard white to light pink. If you look off-season, you can get them for around $10. What a steal!

If you have any other tips and suggestions, please contact me!

The 3 Steps For Building An Empire

I used to play *Age of Empires* a lot, and one thing I loved about the game was the concept of building my own empire. Growing up, I dreamed of becoming an investment banker with an incredible network of buddies, friends, and contacts who I would do business with. "Name a company, a city, or a club and I know someone there" was the thought process I emulated. But instead of building my network, I like to think of it as building my empire.

I've noticed that young women who want to go into business typically don't think about building empires. Instead, they prioritize working hard and learning a lot. I want to change that. **Building an empire should be the first thing on your list.** Why? Because you're going to work hard anyway and because *business isn't just about work. It's about building first class relationships*. At the end of the day, I won't care how many models I've built or how many pitches I've created. I will care about who I survived my summer with and the insane amounts of fun we had. Who knows what kind of business ventures I'll do with my buddies in the future?

3 Steps To Build An Empire:

1. **Network!** Get visible, meet people, make friends, get their contact information.
2. **Unite!** Get everyone to join you on projects or on weekend excursions. Be at the center of your group's social life.
3. **Conquer!** I'll talk about conquering more when we get there.

1. Network

Use every opportunity you have to meet people. The firm will have many **social events** from happy hours to 5K races to community service events–**go to all of them.** Events are a great way to enjoy yourself and do business at the same time. If you're a junior person, which I suspect you are, these events are great places to **meet senior management** in a relaxed setting.

One piece of advice I've given in a previous article is to dress like a boss and wear a full suit to work. This rule doesn't apply to socializing. Unless you literally just came from the office, **leverage your looks** by dressing to look pretty at these events. **People like being around attractive women,** especially when they're having fun. Dressing beautifully will increase your retention rate. I recommend striking a happy middle by wearing a **dress and a blazer.** Feel free to test it out yourself–go to a social event in a full suit and see how many texts, calls, and invites you get from people you just met. Then go to a social event in your nice clothes and see how many texts, calls, and invites you get– compare your results.

Network, network, network! Close the deal, make the ask, and get people's numbers so you can move on to part 2.

2. Unite

Now it's time to **initiate** your own social activities. It's time to put yourself at the center and pull everyone. I can't emphasize how important it is to be socially connected. **Choose the bar, choose the time, and invite everyone**. Don't wait for someone else to do it. **Follow up** and make sure your buddies come along–even if you have to pull them away from their desks. Everyone wants to hang out somewhere Friday and Saturday nights, but many don't make the effort to find a place and round everyone up. If pick a spot, set a time, and invite everyone to the party, people will gravitate toward that.

In getting everyone together to go places, you'll soon be the go-to person for social events on the weekends. This is exactly what you want to achieve when building your empire.

3. Conquer

Kick ass. Win. Conquer. This is "Erin-speak" for "**stay confident and in charge** And that's it. **Network, unite people, and conquer.** The more you do it, the better you'll get at it.

The 90-Hour Work Week: 5 Recommendations For Maintaining The Pace

Before you start your investment banking internship you need to stop and think about how you'll meet that demands of a **90-hour work week**, because that is what you'll face. You will be expected to start work early each morning and continue until late at night. This is a difficult schedule for anyone, even those in great shape. You need to find a way to **stay focused and productive** all day long.

5 Recommendations For Maintaining The Pace:

1. **Eat healthfully.** Don't settle for junk food– it can make you sluggish. Take a daily vitamin. Drink a lot of water to stay **hydrated.**
2. **Sleep.** You will be sleep deprived to a certain degree. When you get home at night, go to sleep right away. The more deeply you sleep at night the more rested you will be in the morning. Do things the same way each week so you won't get distracted; you'll be much more productive.
3. **Take a couple breaks.** Take a food break during the day so that you are not starving all day long. Take a stress-relieving break to go running for a half an hour or do some yoga or whatever helps **rejuvenate** you.
4. **Get to know the people you work with** so that you have a **friendship** relationship with them. Working with people you like and are friends with will make the whole process a lot easier and more enjoyable. The time will fly by because you'll enjoy it.
5. **Go out with friends** and have a good time on weekends. Don't think about work or talk about it too much with your friends. Thinking about other things will help you feel fresh when you do go in to work.

An investment banking internship is an exciting and challenging opportunity. To get the most out it, you need to **take good care of yourself** mentally and physically. If you do, you'll be much better prepared to work full time in the industry. It's important to avoid major burnout. This can make you drag through your work days rather than be productive and driven. While you are doing your internship, keep in mind that this should be your only focus.

Interviews

"The investment banking interview is all about
performance under pressure."

How To Ace The Investment Banking Internship Interview

Once you have been successful **networking** and you have an investment banking **interview**, you need to make sure that you ace it.

The interview process typically starts with your meeting with 2 people from the firm for 30 minutes. The **initial interview** is mostly a "see if you fit" interview. **In other words, they want to see if you are easy to talk to, what your personality is like, and how you handle yourself in the interview.** You also may get a few technical questions about the industry thrown at you in the first interview, so be prepared.

If they like you in the first interview, you'll be asked back for a **second interview** where you'll meet with 3 or 4 people in the company. You'll definitely have some technical questions thrown at you during these meetings. **You'll more than likely be judged on not only your technical knowledge, but also your personality.** If you are going to be spending 80 to 90 hours a week with these people, they want to feel that it will be a good working environment.

If you do well during the second interview, you'll likely be given the position. To make sure that you do well in the interview process, you should be **personable and genuine.** When they ask questions like "how did you get interested in this field?" you can give a short sentence answer, but follow it up with a personal story. In the fit part of the interview, they want to get to know your personally. **They are more likely to hire someone they know and like, so personalize your answers.** Go into the interview with a positive attitude.

Another key to acing the interview is to study ahead of time. Get some of the top investment books in the industry and study like your future depends on it, because it does. Make **flash cards** with pertinent financial questions on them. Write the answers to those questions on the back of the cards. Study these questions until you know the answers backward and forward. You may have a deck of 300 or more cards. If you are going to be in this business, you need to be prepared now.

Be prepared. Be personable. Be positive.

Difficult Banking Interview Questions: What To Expect And How To Prepare

Banks will generally ask you **2 types of questions**: questions that test your knowledge of finance principles and personal questions that test your knowledge of yourself.

1. Preparing for Finance Questions

The most difficult finance questions they'll ask you will involve **multiple layers of financial knowledge**. The only way to prepare for these types of questions is to have a rock solid understanding of finance, which is something you develop through consistent study.

> I would recommend studying the **Mergers & Inquisitions guide**, which provides a great depth of preparation. It was seriously the best guide ever. It's your best bet for preparing well for the interview.

I tried using another finance study guide, but it really didn't go deep enough.

For example, during your interview, they might ask you to pull something from a DCF model and then use another model to confirm the exact valuation ranges. Then they might follow up and ask you how you'd change your evaluation of something if it were now an acquisition target.

There aren't many guides that will prepare you for in-depth questions like that. So again, I recommend the Mergers & Inquisitions guide.

Questions like those are the hardest questions I knew how to answer back then. Spending a lot of time on **brushing up** on finance is really important.

2. Preparing for Personal Questions

For my own interviews, I generally didn't get hit with any particularly hard questions. I was able to respond fluently to pretty much everything they asked me.

Basically, **you should worry more about really solidifying your finance knowledge** because personal questions tend to be very formulaic and predictable. You should always be able to answer questions like, "Why should we hire you right now? Give me 3 reasons why." You should also be able to justify why you want to enter investment banking in particular.

It's amazing how many people go into an interview without even being able to answer basic questions like that.

Nothing is as harmful to your internship chances as an inability to justify your worth as a worker.

Investment Banking Interview Basics: Types Of Interviews And Questions

The investment banking interview is all about performance under pressure. Can you handle getting machine-gunned left and right with finance questions and then interrupted in the middle of your answers with, "Are you sure about that?"

If you can handle investment banking interviews, you will forever know how to respond smartly in the face of aggression. **You can take that skill anywhere**. The good news is, after making it through banking interviews, nothing will phase you. You'll be sitting there smartly thinking, "Bring it on."

What types of interviews can you expect?

There are 4 standard investment banking interview formats:

1. **Phone Screen:** you'll be called to see if you're worth interviewing in person,;expect both fit and technical questions
2. **Fit Interview:** typically a 30 minute interview with mostly fit questions
3. **Super Day:** typically 3-5 interviews of all degrees of difficulty with fit and technical questions from junior to senior bankers
4. **Dinner Screen:** you'll be invited to a dinner or social event, this way a bank can gauge their pool of candidates in one sitting (from my experience, do not reject this invitation if you're serious about the company because they will automatically reject you if you can't come)

What types of investment banking interview questions can you expect?

Questions generally fall under 5 categories:

1. **Finance questions:** valuation, modeling, accounting concepts
2. **Market questions:** what happened in the markets, where indicators are at, where markets will be in the future and why
3. **Fit questions:** why investment banking, walk me through your resume, greatest strengths and weaknesses, greatest accomplishments
4. **Brainteasers:** to throw you off guard and make the interview more exciting
5. **Company questions:** questions about the bank itself, relevant revenue and EPS figures, recent deals it completed

So how should I prepare for these 4 types of interviews and 5 types of questions?

1. **Finance and Market questions:** I built my universe of finance and market questions from friends and from the *Breaking Into Wall Street Investment Banking Interview Guide*

which in my opinion is the best guide on the market.

2. **Fit questions:** I went to the career center and picked up a couple of interview-question books with answers. I recommend *Best Answers to 201 Most Frequently Asked Interview Questions by Matthew DeLuca.*

3. **Brainteasers:** For brainteasers I bought the book *How to Ace the Brainteaser Interview by John Kador* and another called *Captivating Lateral Thinking Puzzles by Paul Sloane* to get used to thinking aloud in "problem solving mode". You're most likely going to get asked brainteasers if you don't have a quantitative background. I thought I'd get slammed with them but I've never gotten asked a brainteaser in a real interview.

4. **Company questions:** I was often asked questions like, "Tell me about some of the recent deals that our group completed in the technology space?" Or, "What vertical within our group would you like to work in?" Get your mentors to help you with answers to these questions.

Note to the wise–**expect to be grilled every second of every day.** Even if a mentor tells you that you're going to a fit interview you still need to anticipate getting asked the tough finance questions. You can't expect people to stick to the rules because there really aren't any, and the definitions above are already loosely defined. I had phone screens that were supposed to be fit interviews turn out to be machine-gun-round finance-in-your-face interviews. On the flipside, I had super days where I wasn't asked a single finance question. The point is–**be prepared at all times**.

To prepare I made a **flashcards** of every interview question I could expect and organized them by category. In the second part of my preparation strategy, I tried as many investment banking **interview practice sessions** as possible. I needed to get comfortable being put on the spot. I asked my friends in finance, mentors, and career center advisors to help with this. Just do it for 10-15 minutes! Your friends who are also undergoing recruiting are the best partners for this because the practice aids both parties.

By the end of recruiting I had a stack of about **300 flashcards** in each category that I had gone over countless times. My friends and I, who were going through recruiting together, would flashcard each other and get a kick out of being the interviewer, trying to be as brutal as possible. Our over-preparation was critical to getting multiple interviews at and multiple offers from multiple bulge bracket firms. Try it and let me know how it goes!

38 Basic Investment Banking Interview Questions

We use these questions to interview associates in the Blyth Fund, Stanford's student-managed, 6-figure portfolio. Associates need to have a **basic understanding of stock analysis and financial markets.** The questions are mostly definition-oriented and test how well you know basic concepts. Finance interviewers are likely to ask these types of questions to competitive freshmen and sophomores.

Fit Questions:

- What are your greatest strengths?
- Why are you applying for this position?
- What is your greatest weakness?
- Tell us about at time when you had to think on your feet.
- What is a recent book you read?
- Teach me something.
- What was your greatest failure and what did you learn from it?
- Tell me about your previous finance experience.
- Why should we hire you?

Finance Basics:

At this level, you're only expected to know what the below "definition terms" are, as opposed to having to explain their role in valuation and their underlying relationships. Wikipedia can be a great resource for some of these questions.

- Walk me through the 3 financial statements.
- Walk me through the income statement.
- What's the difference between revenue and net income?
- What is EBITDA?
- What is the basic balance sheet formula?
- How is the cash flow statement organized?
- What is working capital?
- What is the P/E ratio?
- What is a mutual fund?
- What is an option?
- What is a bond?
- What is the relationship between a bond's price and yield and why?
- What is an ETF?

Market Questions:

- Where is the Dow at?

- Where is the S&P at?
- Tell me about a stock you follow, where its price is today and what its price was yesterday.
- Tell me about a recent article you read in the paper and how you would make a trade off of that article.
- Pitch me a stock.
- Pitch me another stock.
- What are some points that refute the pitch you just made?
- What stocks and market sectors do you follow?
- Teach me about how to analyze investments in XYZ sector.
- Where do you see markets going next year?

Economics Questions:

- How does the Fed conduct monetary policy?
- What is the Federal Fund's rate?
- If interest rates rise, what does that imply for the future of the economy?
- What happens to American currency when inflation rises?
- What happens to money supply when interest rates rise?

If you can readily answer these questions, you should be able to handle anything your investment banking interviewer will ask you.

62 Advanced Investment Banking Interview Questions

These are questions that we use to interview Directors of the Blyth Fund, Stanford's student managed 6-figure portfolio. Directors are members with 1 year of experience who have led several stock pitches, are voting members of the board, and are the leaders and teachers in the fund. **These questions are intensely valuation oriented and a lot of them require deeper thought and explanation.** I find these questions to fit perfectly well with the types of questions very competitive juniors and seniors are likely to get asked in finance interviews. If you can answer these questions and if you understand the interrelationships between these financial concepts, you'll be totally set for your interviews. You'll be the pre-trained candidate that banks are looking for.

Valuation Questions:

1. What are the three ways you can value a company?
2. Walk me through a Discounted Cash Flow (DCF) model.
3. What is the formula for Free Cash Flow?
4. What is the formula for Weighted Average Cost of Capital (WACC)?
5. What is the difference between levered & unlevered free cash flow?
6. How do you calculate enterprise value?
7. What is the difference between enterprise value and equity value?
8. What is working capital and why do you add the change in working capital to FCF?
9. What is the present value formula?
10. Why would you lever and unlever beta?
11. What comps would you use in a comps model to value companies in X sector?
12. Why would you use EV/Revenue comps when we can use EV/EBIT?
13. Why would a ratio like EV/Net Income not make sense?
14. How is a company's capital structure different from its operating structure?
15. How do you calculate Cash Flow from Operations on the Cash Flow Statement?
16. Why does an increase in an asset decrease Cash Flow from Operations? In your explanation, explain the link to working capital.
17. Why does an increase in a liability increase Cash Flow from Operations? In your explanation, explain the link to working capital.
18. What is the CAPM model?
19. What is the link between the balance sheet and the cash flow statement?
20. What's the difference between expensing and capitalizing?
21. In which financial statements does Net Income appear?
22. Run me through the three financial statements if depreciation increased by $10.
23. When would you not use a DCF to value a company? What would you use in its place?
24. Walk me through the treasury method.

25. Where would you find total number of shares outstanding of a company?
26. If you could only bring one financial statement with you, on an island, which would it be?
27. How do you select comparable companies when putting together a comps model?
28. How do you know if your DCF is too dependent on future assumptions?
29. Should the cost of equity be higher for a $5bn or $500mm mkt cap company?
30. Will WACC be higher for a $5bn or $500mm mkt cap company?
31. What is the Gordon Growth terminal value formula?

Market Questions:

1. Where is the Dow at?
2. Where is the S&P at?
3. Tell me about a stock you follow, where its price is today and what its price was yesterday.
4. Tell me about a recent article you read in the paper and how you would make a trade off of that article.
5. Pitch me a stock.
6. Pitch me another stock.
7. Now how would you hedge that pitch you just made?
8. What are some points that refute the pitch you just made?
9. What stocks / sector do you follow?
10. Teach me about how to analyze investments in XYZ sector.
11. Where do you see markets going next year?
12. Tell me about two companies that should merge together and why.

Economics Questions:

1. How does the Fed conduct monetary policy?
2. What is the relationship between inflation and interest rates?
3. If the federal funds rate decreases, does this weaken or strengthen the dollar?
4. If bond spreads are increasing, what does this tell you about the state of the economy?
5. If the dollar weakens, what happens to company earnings?
6. What happens to the strength of currency when inflation rises?
7. What happens to inflation, interest rates, and bond prices when the dollar weakens against the yen?
8. Say the USD strengthens. What happens to: earnings, inflation, and interest rates?
9. Say the USD weakens. What happens to: earnings, inflation, and interest rates?
10. Tell me about some economic indicators that you follow and where they're trending.
11. What is the effect of inflation on bond prices and why?

Portfolio Questions:

1. When you add a risky stock to a portfolio that's already risky how is the overall portfolio affected?

2. If the CEO of a company states that his stock is doing well and has gone up 20% in the past 12 months, is the company actually doing well?
3. If you read that a given mutual fund performed 50% ROI in the past year, would you invest in it?
4. Should I add XYZ stock to the Blyth Fund portfolio?
5. What does a correlation coefficient of -1, 1, and 0 mean?

Options Questions:

1. What's the difference between a call and a put?
2. What's the difference between a naked and a covered call?
3. Why would we want to buy an option instead of buying/shorting a stock?
4. How might we be able to hedge a position with options?

Have A Low GPA? Tell Your Story.

In banking, a low GPA, or anything less than a 3.5-4.0, is a red flag.

Bankers will question your ability to handle work. It could very well hurt your candidacy.

My Perspective on GPA:

I personally think GPA is a terrible indicator of how well you can do on the job. I'd much rather investigate what the candidate's greatest achievements are, what they're passionate about, and things that actually shed light on the person's ability to succeed.

Moreover, a **terrible GPA** can be the result of hundreds of things other than slacking off in class. For example, you could have taken a series of really challenging classes. Or, you could be working part-time at a finance firm to pay for school. Or, you could be starting and managing your own business while taking challenging classes.

GPA alone does not tell your story. If it's high, it doesn't mean you're a rockstar. And if it's low, it doesn't mean you're going to fail in life. **It's all about your story.**

How to Handle the Interview Question, *Why is your GPA so low?*

So, I had a 3.3 GPA when I was recruiting as a junior. And I got asked this question all the time. But, instead of it being an awkward moment that I was always trying to avoid, I turned my answer into a big victory story.

Think about why you actually have a low GPA. Is it because you took 10 math classes and are inherently terrible at math? Is it because for a year you started your own company and were focusing on growing it instead of studying all day? Is it because you spend 20 hours a week working part-time to pay for college loans? Is it because you have a 2 year old younger sister that you're helping your single mother take care of when you're home from school? Give it some thought.

Usually, most people have a low GPA not because they're inherently lazy and incompetent, but because they decided to prioritize something else in their lives. Think about what it was that you prioritized and craft your answer around it. If you achieved what you prioritized at the expense of your GPA, more power to you!

You want to structure your answer like this, *I may have a low GPA but at that time in life I was trying to achieve 2 things. First, I failed calculus in high school and wanted to turn that around when I came to Stanford. So I took 10 math classes from introduction to calculus to differential equations and intermediate econometrics. I didn't ace every class, but I faced my fear of numbers and now you can hit me with any mathematical problem and I will solve it. Second, I took up a part-time internship at Houlihan Lokey to pay for my student loans and become financially independent. I was working 15 hours a week learning how to build comps models and pitch books and balancing work and school was one of the most challenging and rewarding experiences in my life. I may not have had the best GPA that quarter, but I learned what it's like to support myself and gain financial independence and I'm forever equipped with that skill set in life.*

Now you see, this person may have a 3.0 GPA, but she did ace the interview. Not only that, but given her story, she sounds like she has more dimensions and more resilience than someone who took it easy.

Practice telling it every day until you can tell it flawlessly and articulately – you might actually evoke emotion from your interviewer! The more you tell a story the better you get at telling it, so make sure you practice this one. The next time someone asks you, *why is your GPA so low*, tell them your story. Your victory story.

Tell A Story: "Why Investment Banking?"

You enter the interview room, shake hands with the two well-suited people on the other end of the table, and have a seat. One of the interviewers folds his hands, leans back in his chair and asks you, "So why do you want to go into investment banking?"

So how should you craft your answer? Simple. **Tell it as a story with a beginning, a turning point, and an end**.

Answers are boring. Stories, on the other hand, are engaging and multi-dimensional, especially if tell them well. Many people who ace the interview are people who are good storytellers. Practice your storytelling! Starting out your answer with, "Well I want to do finance because I'm good at trading" isn't as engaging as, "It started out when I made $3000 one Tuesday morning on a trade." See what I mean? Turn your answers into **3-5 sentence short stories** with a beginning, a turning point or *aha*! moment, and an end.

1. The Beginning

What sparked your interest in finance? Was it a news article? Was it a classmate who told you about the exciting weeks and big-deal transactions? Was it an econ class or a student group? Was it when you accomplished something in a finance or business-like field like raising or making thousands of dollars?

Pinpoint where it all started and use that moment of awakening as the beginning of your story.

2. The Turning Point

The turning point, or the *aha* **moment** is the moment the light bulb went off in your head and you realized, "Wow! This is amazing. I want to do this for a living." When was that moment? Was it when you attempted and completed your first financial model? Was it when you aced a stock pitch that you made in front of your investing club? Was it when you won a case study or stock pitch competition? Was it when you were already in the middle of a previous internship and were working on one of the biggest deals in the sector?

Transition from your beginning to your turning point and then from your turning point to your ending.

3. The Ending

The conclusion of your answer, **the ending**, can be many things. It can be, "And that's why I decided to apply with this division of the company, I want to experience what it's like to be a tech banker in the heart of Silicon Valley." Or it can be, "And so because of these sales-like successes I decided that I wanted to seek a fast-paced and high-intensity environment like the sales desk." Or even, "I knew for sure I wanted to explore highly quantitative trading methods after I aced my advanced econometrics class and that's why I'm interviewing with you today."

Your ending can be a conclusion of certainty like "and that's why I want to do sales and trading" or it can be a more open-ended stepping point like "and that's why I'm interviewing with you today, I want to explore this new opportunity." You don't have to be certain about your exact next career move, you just have to know why what you're interviewing for is in the conclusion of your story. Is it your perfect post-college job? Is it your perfect next step? Is it something exciting that you'd like to explore for a quarter?

Putting it All Together

So why do you want to do investment banking?

Let's review. First, tell a story. Begin with **the moment that piqued your interest** in finance. Transition to the **turning point or aha moment** you had when you realized why, genuinely and deep down inside, you want to do this. End with the reason **why you're sitting in the interview room**.

Now take a break, open a new word document, and begin crafting your answer.

3 Interview Techniques For Women In Business

Perhaps You've Wondered, "Will I Be Interviewed Differently Because I'm A Woman Wanting To Break Into Banking?" Or Have You Asked Yourself, "Should I Act Differently? Should I Be More Professional?"

I wouldn't say females are interviewed differently because *everyone gets asked the same questions*. But, I'd say psychologically, **the interviewer will have a different response to a female's answers**, personality, and behavior than they would to a male with the same answers, personality, and behavior.

In fact, I think **women can leverage 3 things to really stand above many male candidates**: over-preparing and over-delivering, disarming them with your smile, and leveraging your looks.

1. Over-Prepare and Over-Deliver

Over-prepare and over-deliver. You can never stop over-preparing. The last thing you want is to be the only woman in an interview group and to not know an answer to a basic question like, "Walk me through the three financial statements."

What constitutes over-preparing? How do you know you're preparing hard enough?

You should be practicing for interviews for at least 3+ hours per day during recruiting season. You should be constantly reviewing your finance and practicing telling your stories so that you could ace your interview in your sleep.

You want to impress your interviewers by being *better* than all the male candidates. You need to have your finance down, backwards and forwards, inside and out. No slacking!

2. Disarm Them With Your Smile

Think about it. Your interviewers are likely going to be males who sit at their cubicles with their fellow males all day long and stare at Excel spreadsheets. Okay, maybe its not that bad–but they don't get too much regular interaction with the outside world.

Now imagine you walk in for an interview, shake hands, and they throw a really tough finance question at you. You answer it confidently and smoothly and then to top it off, *you smile*! **You smile because you just nailed the question**. And, you smile because you also want to warm up your interviewer to you!

This is a powerful technique. I'm not saying you need to be flirtatious or that you should have a creepy, toothy grin. No. I'm saying, when you have the opportunity, smile! Make the interview fun instead of a machine-gun-finance-in-your-face massacre. **Smiling confidently and happily** at your interviewer after answering touch questions will totally disarm him.

Plus, how often does a smart and pretty girl smile at him on a day to day basis?

3. Leverage Your Looks

Be an enthusiastic, glowing source of energy. Many recommend "being confident" but I say **go beyond confidence– be confident** and fun to be around. Positivity and smiling are *big* things in your favor. It's much better to be confident, energetic, and a pleasure to be around than just confident.

Also – look your prettiest. *I say this carefully*. Please don't misinterpret it! Leverage your looks as best you can. **Every woman is beautiful**. Don't hide your beauty because you think you're being more professional. If you have beautiful eyes, make them come alive with eyeliner and mascara. If you have beautiful hair, let it down, don't tie it up!

Here's what not to do: *Don't always dress "strictly business"* by wearing my thick-rimmed glasses, tying your hair up in a bun, not wearing any jewelry, and only wearing a full black suit & white collared shirt to interviews and networking events. Instead of being awesome and fun to be around, you're quiet and serious and always talking about business because you're trying to be professional. Bad.

First, you're not going to be fun to hang around. Second, **you're going to look like Miss Trunchbull**. You don't want to look like that.

Instead, what you want to achieve is being respected as a professional woman and actually making friends and meeting people who are receptive and warm to you. Leverage your looks and your inherently fun and energetic personality!

If you want, test it out. Go to an event where you're dressed "too professional." See who gets in touch with you *professionally* afterward. Then go to an event where you're dressed professional but where you also leverage your looks. I bet you'll instantly notice a difference.

The Investment Banking Interview Process

After networking and scheduling an interview with an investment banking firm, you have to prepare for your interview.

You should have been preparing for the interview way before you actually get it. You should have been studying the top books on investment banking all along, once you decided that this was what you wanted to do for a living. Make sure that your knowledge of the investment banking terminology is excellent. Studying should be an ongoing process.

When you get your initial interview with an investment bank there will likely be 2 people that you meet with for about 30 minutes the first time. **This interview is probably going to be more of a "will this person fit into our organization" interview.** They will want to find out about your personality. You will likely be with these people for 80 to 90 hours a week. They want to make sure they can deal with you and get along with you. In this first interview you may be asked some technical questions pertaining to the industry so don't be surprised and be prepare even on this interview with your technical knowledge. If you don't know an answer to a question in this session, don't fake it. Be honest and tell them that you don't know it. Otherwise they will note your dishonesty.

If the people from the first interview like you, you'll probably be asked back for a second interview. This one will be a bit longer. You will likely talk to 3 or 4 different people in the company. **These meetings may be strictly technical or they may be a fit and technical interview combined. They want to know that you will be a good fit and that you know something about the business.** Again, if you don't know the answer to a question, don't fake an answer. They can tell you are not sincere and this will hurt your chances of getting a job offer.

If your second interview with the 3 or 4 people goes well, the company will likely call you and offer you the job.

The Fit Interview: 4 Tips

First of all, what is the fit part of the interview? **It's the personality part of the meeting.** The people doing this part of the interview want to see if they could get along with you. They want to see if you are genuinely interested in the business and their company. You'll be spending a lot of time with your co-workers so if you're phony or stuck up, you won't get too far. You want to let them see who you really are.

4 Pieces Of Advice For The Fit Interview:

1. **Be prepared** for the technical as well as the fit part of the interview. You'll feel more confident.

2. **Be honest** with your interviewers. They appreciate honesty. Lying won't bode well. If there's a question you don't know, tell them you don't know but will learn more about the topic.

3. **Let your interviewers get to know you personally.** Become friends with them. People like to hire friend; if you can establish yourself as friendly and a good person to be around, you'll take a big step toward an internship.

4. **Personalize your answers.** If you are asked to describe your greatest strength, you can give the short sentence answer to start with, like "I am very smart, people-oriented and driven," but everyone gives this answer. Tell something that happened to you that made you realize that this was your strength or something that helped you develop this strength. Giving a canned answer to a question without personalizing it won't give you an advantage. Let them see you as a unique individual, not a person reciting the correct answers.

In the investment banking business, your personality is extremely important. You deal with a lot of people at your company every day. If you get into the business long term, your dealings with people outside the firm will also be a major indication of whether or not you are successful. Personality is huge. The business is important too, but that's something you can learn over time. Your personality has to fit.

Investment Banking Internship

"There are hundreds of alternatives to the traditional investment banking bulge bracket internship."

6 Tips For Internship Success

After you have put so much effort into networking to get interviews and then doing well in the interviews so that you get hired, you want to follow remember some important tips for doing well while you are in your internship.

6 Things To Remember:

1. **Work hard.** Obviously.
2. **Ask your manager for the hard work.** You want to use this experience to get into the real grit of the investment banking business. If you don't ask, your manager may give you the small jobs. When you finish your internship, you want to have gained as much knowledge as possible so that you might get hired permanently after you finish school.
3. **Be sociable.** Get to know the other people in the firm. Make sure that they know your name and who you are. Don't just be the person who sits in a cubical and works like crazy. If they know you personally, you'll do much better.
4. **Find a way to relieve your stress and renew your mind every day.** You might go for a 30 minute run or do yoga for 30 minutes or whatever you like to do. This will help you refocus and push hard when you get back to your desk.
5. **Eat a healthy diet.** You'll have an easier time staying focused.
6. **Talk to the people in the elevator.** Ask them what they do at the company or how they are. After seeing them a few times, you'll become friends. This will help you make an impression.

To summarize, **work hard** and **ask for the difficult work** to show your drive and interest in the business. Let your managers know that you want to handle the big issues and show them you can handle them well. You're doing an internship to get some great experience working in the business, so go for it. Besides working hard, it is critical that you **socialize.** Get to know the people you are working with well. You'll leave a better impression and learn a lot from listening to their stories and experiences. If you do both of these things well, your internship will have be a success.

Busy Schedule? Prioritize Your Preparation

First of all, you should know that getting an internship at a top bank takes a lot of time and effort preparing. **If you're not willing to put in a lot of time, you're not going to get the internship.** It's that simple.

However, if you do find yourself in a position where you only have a limited amount of prep time and are looking to prioritize, you should concentrate on studying for finance and preparing for advanced interview questions. Some banks will just interview you to see how well you fit. For many banks, though, **your knowledge of finance** will be their main concern.

Practice with the interview format in mind. Make **flashcards** of the tough questions you think your interviewer might ask and study those whenever you have a chance. Everybody has breaks from time to time. A few minutes is all it takes to look over a couple of flashcards and practice some of your answers.

10 Alternatives To An Investment Banking Internship

You're probably a college student looking for a way to eventually land a nice bulge bracket stint by the time you graduate. Most students think, "I'll just drop my resume and cover letter by the career center with the major bulge brackets and hopefully get interviews."

What if this doesn't work? What's your back-up plan?

10 Great Alternatives To Investment Banking Internships

1. Apply to middle-market and boutique investment banks.
2. Work for a Hedge funds.
3. Find work at a Venture capital fund.
4. Work with private wealth management groups.
5. Apply for a position at an investment management group.
6. Work for a corporate finance division at a company like Disney.
7. Work at a financial services corporation like Visa, Mastercard, PayPal, or Bling.
8. Join a start-up or non-profit where you'll be trusted with fundraising and money-making responsibilities.
9. Travel to a village in Africa to implement a financial-economic system and invest in the businesses you believe have potential.
10. Start your own company that will revolutionize the financial services sector and aim to be revenue positive by the end of summer.

Regardless of whether you land an internship at a big investment bank, you can do something awesome this summer. Don't give up if your Plan A fails. Don't languish in the library studying for summer classes when you can be out there making things happen. There are hundreds of alternatives to the traditional investment banking bulge bracket internship. Starting out with these 10 alternatives just might open up doors and opportunities for you that you've never dreamed of.

Your Secret Opportunity: Middle Market Investment Banking

Many students chase the prestigious bulge bracket investment banks in pursuit of elite summer internships that might turn into full time offers. But what if you're a freshman or sophomore who was rejected from all the investment banks? What if you live in a small city that doesn't have bulge bracket divisional offices? What if you're someone who will be happy simply working at any investment bank?

Good news. There are hundreds of middle market and boutique investment banks you should consider pursuing. These businesses offer a stellar opportunity because you can get very close to the same experience no matter what level you are.

How do I know this?

Well, when I was a sophomore, I was set on getting an investment banking internship and nothing short of that. I went through recruiting, sent my resume to all the big banks, and got rejected by every single one of them. (Side note: at that time I didn't know how to network so no wonder I got rejected). I then sent my resume to all the freshman, sophomore, and women's diversity programs at the bulge brackets and got rejected from all of those too!

I then thought, "Ok somewhere in the world there must be a small investment bank that's dying to have an intern. I have to find that bank."

So I scoured Google and found that there were tons of small investment banks all over the world. Tons. That's when I learned about boutique investment banks (small banks that typically specialize in a sector and provide advisory services) and middle market investment banks (banks that focus on smaller corporate clients with roughly $100mm to under $1bn in revenue).

I targeted banks in San Francisco and made a record of all the ones that I liked in a spreadsheet. And then I bombarded them with emails. Each email had my cover letter in the body with my resume and a stock pitch as attachments. I sent out 200+ emails and followed up on 100+ banks. Within a month of this persistence, four banks got back to me, and I ended up working at one of them.

If you are in a similar position, instead of turning away from getting a job or giving up altogether, work hard and aim for a boutique or middle market stint. It's well worth your efforts especially if you're set on pursuing this career. Remember– somewhere in the world there is a small investment bank that's dying to have you as their intern. You have to find that bank!

Trust: The Secret To Success In Investment Banking

When I started my first banking internship I believed that I needed to work really hard to get on the major deals and be successful. So for a good 7 weeks, that's all I did! I worked really hard. I was at my desk cranking on something all the time. **I believed that sooner or later, someone was going to notice**, and that my work product would be so good that I'd automatically get put on the big deals.

That was far from the truth.

There was another intern there who seemed to never work and was **always socializing**. He basically walked around the floor every day and just talked to everybody. He kept getting on good projects and I thought, "What? But he doesn't do anything!"

It perplexed and bothered me so much that I went to my **analyst** and I asked, "Okay, hypothetical scenario. Let's say you're starting a company. Guy A is your buddy and doesn't really work very hard. Guy B is someone you work with who isn't really your buddy but works very hard. Who will you start your company with?"

My analyst looked at me like the answer was obvious and said, "I'd pick my buddy any day of the week."

I said, "What?! But he doesn't work hard."

My analyst said, "True– but **a buddy is someone I can trust.** The hypothetical person that works hard– I don't know them and so I can't trust them."

Big lesson here. If you're starting a business, **you want to do business with someone who you know has your back**. If you're the analyst and have two interns to delegate work to, would you delegate work to the intern who does a stellar job on the projects and makes the effort to reach out and get to know you or would you delegate work to the machine in the corner of the room who seemingly only cares about finishing work? The answer should be obvious.

What's the solution? Start socializing. Get to know people. **Develop relationships** that transcend the pitch book you're working on.

It may take awhile to sink in, but give this one some thought. You're not just here to work. You're here to build relationships that last even when work is over. Why? Because businesses aren't built on pillars of **hard work** alone. They're built on the foundation of trust with pillars of hard work to drive the business forward. **Trust trumps hard work any day of the week.**

Choosing The Right Major: What A Major Will Do For You

Some people think a major in college should directly translate to a future job. If you want to be a doctor, you should be a biology major. If you want to work with a tech company, you should be an engineering or computer science major. If you want to be an investment banker, you should major in finance or economics. And if you're majoring in English, Art, or Film, good luck!

Well, here's the good news– it no longer works that way. There are jobs that are skill-specific, but **banking, consulting, and most anything in business isn't that way because everything that's important is learned on the job**. It's helpful to have some knowledge of accounting, financial math, and markets, but it's not a prerequisite.

What's the point of a major if it's not going to train you for your future job?

1. The major will teach you how to **think critically** and **solve problems**
2. The major will give you a sector-specific body of knowledge and **skill set**
3. You'll get to **meet** and spend your time with people in that major who will shape your college experience

Your major will not prepare you for your job. **Your job will prepare you for your job.**

Then how do you choose a major?

1. Ask yourself– what are my passions? Where do my skills lie? What skills do I want to learn? What major can provide the intersection of these 3 things: **passions, skills, and the new skills to learn**?
2. **Audit higher-level classes** of your intended major. Get involved, don't just *guess* what your major should be based on the classes you took freshman year. See what it's like – what are the students like? What are the professors like? Ask yourself, "Do I want to be like this in a couple years?" If you like what you see, if it piques your interest and excitement, that's a good sign. If on the other hand, things are looking pretty grim, don't expect them to magically change by the time you're a junior because they won't!
3. **Talk to juniors and especially seniors** of your intended major. Ask to see their problem sets, their notebooks, their best projects. Ask them about **their experience** as a whole, what classes they thought were the best, and what classes to avoid and why. To avoid sampling bias, talk to a lot of seniors and juniors to get truly **diverse perspectives and opinions.**

You can always get entrepreneurial and **design your own major.** What if you like Chinese + Finance + International Relations all bundled into a major? Design it. What if you like Medieval Studies + Accounting + Chemistry? Do it! What about Computer Science + Italian +

Economics? You can also do bundles of multiple majors and minors– like a major in Engineering and a double minor in Film and Ballroom Dancing. Or a double major in Art and Computer Science and a minor in Arabic.

A lot of these **seemingly unrelated** fields can lend themselves to amazing skills that transcend *boring* "traditional" majors:

1. **Chinese + Finance + International Relations =** Build a company founded in China that connects the Chinese economy to the world economy to alleviate poverty.
2. **Medieval Studies + Accounting + Chemistry =** Invent a chemical product using modern day chemistry and old school alchemy texts and turn it into a business via accounting knowledge.
3. **Fashion + Italian + Economics =** Work with an investment bank in Milan and lead deals with companies at the center of luxury and high-end fashion.

How do you think candidates that pursue their multiple interests stand out compared to *plain vanilla Econ majors*?

Creativity is possible. I simply encourage you to think about your major beyond how it can prepare you for your job and to craft and design your college experience in a way that lets you have your cake and eat it too.

The 3 Keys To Client Management

People love it when you take care of their problems. Client management, for interns, takes care of your boss's problems.

3 Keys To Client Management:

1. Prepare

Before throwing in the towel at night, review what needs to be done for all your deals tomorrow and over the next week. You need to know this. Not just the stuff you were assigned, but all the stuff that needs to be done for the client. **Take ownership of the deal.** Take responsibility over all of its aspects because you're just as important to the deal as your VP is. The review process will take you **30 minutes** now, but it will save badly timed *surprises* tomorrow. Instead of waiting for your VP to tell you what to do, report to him first thing in the morning, update him on next step and what needs to be done. If you don't know what the next step is, ask and remember for the next time.

2. Put Out Fires

I've received my fair share of some pretty sharp emails (some sent only to me, others sent to the whole deal team). Clients come to you like this when you haven't updated them in a while, when you make a mistake on a memo and they think you're trying to dupe them, when they don't understand what's going on, and when they feel like they're not being taken care of. It makes sense; **they're paying good money and they expect to be treated well.**

If you're the recipient of one of these emails, first **take ownership,** then **take initiative**. If you made a mistake or if something wasn't clear, take ownership, **fix the problem** and **update them** asking if you can help with anything else. Second, take initiative. If the client feels like the team isn't updating them enough, then update them yourself when progress is made on your end. If you're working with a VP who wants to approve everything before you do it, run your draft email by them before sending. If you're working with a VP who wants you to take initiative, then just cc the VP on the email.

3. Take Calls

I could count on getting the same reaction every single time: "You've been talking to clients on the phone– as an intern?!" **To outperform as an intern, you have to perform like an analyst.** On deal memos and documents that were sent out, I'd offer my contact information so that I'd be first point of contact for one-off questions. In addition, I made a **deal sheet** that had answers to commonly asked questions for each of my deals, so when I received a call, I could easily answer questions. If I didn't know the answer I'd say, "I don't know that off the top of my head– but I can definitely email you the answer, if that's all right?"

If you want to manage your clients well (and you should be managing them well even though you're "just an intern"), **be prepared to take calls and answer questions on the deal by anyone at any point of the day**. You don't have to memorize a bunch of numbers, just make a deal sheet with all your numbers on it and have that by your desk. When you pick up the phone, answer confidently and make it clear that you're the person's side and want to help him or her out. If you don't know the answer, then check with your VP and call back. **Act as if you were a full time analyst** and **take care of your clients.**

Read To Get Ahead: My Bookshelf Of Business Books

Introductory Books on Finance and Accounting:

Get the *The Wall Street Journal Complete Money & Investing Guidebook* if you're looking for an introduction to the field that's like white wine–dry and refined. It tastes pretty good but☐ you have to used to it. Get the *S&P Guide to Money and Investing* if you're looking for fun, picture-book overview of the financial markets. The *Financial Business Box* is a colorful introduction to accounting, Excel, and financial math made fun again in picture-book style. It's☐ the same guide that was given to the summer analyst class at J.P. Morgan.

Interview Preparation:

Get *How to Ace the Brainteaser Interview* if you're looking to refine and master the art of☐ answering brainteasers, guesstimates, and intimidating questions suavely and with style. I recommend *Best Answers to 201 Most Frequently Asked Interview Questions* if you're looking to understand what's behind the interview question and how to spin your story in different ways to get your most desired traits across to your interviewer. It's a solid, basic guide.

I recommend *301 Best Questions to ASK On Your Interview* if you really want to impress your interviewer. At the end of the interview, they'll open it up for questions. That's a golden opportunity. That's when you blow them away with your well-prepared and well-researched questions and when you differentiate yourself from all the other candidates who didn't have anything to ask.

Job Preparation and Networking:

There aren't a lot of books written on job preparation and networking, but I found *They Don't Teach Corporate in College* to be a handy, calming guide to the new workplace environment. The work-place does not revolve around sitting at your desk all day and cranking on a spreadsheet; it revolves around people. Read *Never Eat Alone* to learn how meaningful networking really is and how to get good at it.

Although getting an MBA is probably far away for most of us, I found *How to Get into the Top MBA Programs* to be an incredible find. It sheds a lot of light and insight on what business☐ schools look for and what the most competitive, top-notch candidates are like. I enjoyed reading it and aspired to new heights.

Investing Books:

Investing books? But I want to do investment banking! Well, take a step back. What do investment bankers do? They provide financial products and services like mergers and☐

aquisitions, initial public offerings, equity and debt financing, and advisory work. But what does it take to provide those services? What's at the *core* of knowing how to engineer a merger, how to take a company public, or how much debt you need to raise? Valuation. You need to know what the company is worth! How do you value a company? There are many ways, but you typically make some kind of financial model.

Investors look for companies to put their money in. They have to know valuation. If you want to understand how to value a company, you'll want to understand how to do so from a fundamental *and* technical perspective. I built my understanding of fundamental valuation by reading investing books written by the masters – **Graham, Fisher, Lynch, and Greenblatt.** You should too.

Don't know where to start? Go for *The Warren Buffett Way* or *The Little Book that Beats the Market* because they're easy-to-read and process. Before you know it you'll be moving on to the more nuanced *Intelligent Investor* and *One Up on Wall Street*!

The Little Book Series:

Another way you can immerse yourself with finance is to read *all* of the Little Book Series. Colleagues at the Blyth Fund are big fans of these books because they're quick, informative reads that you can complete in short sitting. They're all written by amazing people. Check them out!

Accounting, Finance, Money and Banking Textbooks:

Accounting is the single most important foundation you need to build before going into finance. You can learn it on the job, but it's going to save you a lot of pain and frustration if you master the art beforehand. You don't need to be a CFA, but you need to understand what the financial statements are and how you're going to use them to value a company. I learned accounting in class with the *Financial Accounting* textbook by doing all the practice problems.

If you want to understand financial instruments like stocks, bonds, and options and investing theory like CAPM and APT then you'll want to check out *Investments*. The *Investments* book is a business school level introductory book that gets pretty technical and mathy. Again, do all the problems in the back of the book and build your in-deth and in-the-weeds understanding of how these financial instruments work. Before you know it, you'll start trading them!

If you want to learn what a bank is, what its place is amongst other financial institutions, and how the whole financial ecosystem works, check out *Economics of Money, Banking, and Financial Markets*. The book is very soft, not a lot of technical or math work. Just a sweeping (and somewhat dry) introduction to how financial markets work and how all the pieces of the puzzle fit together.

Advanced Investment Banking and Business Books:

Looking for a more advanced treatment of higher-level finance concepts? You don't have to buy these books to become proficient with these concepts. Most of them were too expensive for me, so I'd just steal away to the bookstore and read them off the shelves at the cafe. If you're looking for a comprehensive list containing the best of the best, this is it. The *Valuation* book is pretty much the bible. It's a bit dry and text-book-y but it has *everything*.

If you want a shortcut, read *The Wall Street MBA,* which I found a lot easier to digest. *Investment Banking* is an overall excellent read. It's the practical version of the valuation guides that keeps academic things to a minimum. Read *Leveraged Finance* if you're looking to pursue an internship with a levfin group. If you're looking for an in-depth treatment of M&A, read *The Art of M & A,* which is 1000 pages long. It doesn't get technical, but it tells you about all the pieces in the puzzle and people's incentives. The book is written in question and answer format so it flows very well. A great complement to that is the *Harvard Business Review on Mergers and Acquisitions,* which is a collection of articles from the magazine.

Personal Business Favorites:

These books are all-time favorites because they've fundamentally changed the way I work and the way I view the world. If you're looking for a total world-view makeover, check out the amusingly titled *How to Win Friends and Influence People.* The book was written in the 1920s by Dale Carnegie, a super-successful, charismatic, and very well networked guy (not to be confused with Andrew Carnegie). If you want to understand how to *do* business, how to really network, and how important people are in your day-to-day business life, the book is a must-read.

Check out *Four Hour Workweek* if you're looking for a way to become an always-vacationing rich dudette without having to be an investment banker. Read *What I Wish I Knew When I Was 20* and *Rework* if you're looking to spice the way you work and think with a little entrepreneurial seasoning.

And of course, definitely read *How to Become CEO* if you want to learn how to act and think like a future leader in the company. I loved *How to Become CEO*! It was short, sweet, and it definitely shows you how to separate yourself from the pack if you have huge long-term visions and want to be a leader.

Investment Banking Internships Are For Passionate People

If you're thinking about getting an investment banking internship, you should be passionate about the industry. This is a tough business and will require many hours of dedication to get a foothold in the industry. You will be working many hours per week, so it is critical that you love your work. That means you must be extremely passionate about the work.

Not only is it important to show this passion while you are working, but you will have to **show your passion during the process** of getting the job. It will be noticed in your attempt to get the interview. It will be noticed during your interviewing process, which will have a major impact on whether or not you get the job. During the time you are working, it will show as well. **If you don't have a passion for the business, it will show.**

You'll be working 80-90 hours a week. If you don't love what you are doing, you will find that getting out of bed in the morning will be very difficult. **If you're driven to learn more and more about the business every day, it will be easy to get up each morning and get to work.** You will potentially talk to clients every day and work in the midst of large business deals. If you have the passion, you will love putting in the time and effort required of you each day.

You'll know when you have the passion; there will be no question. If getting into investment banking is something you really want to do, you won't have to wonder if you're doing the right thing. **Many people try investment banking for the prestige it might bring. If this is why you're considering an internship, you are wasting your time.** You should try to find prestige somewhere else. You won't have the drive to achieve success in the industry. Again, it's hard work and long hours to get to any level of success in the business.

If, however, you think about nothing else and have a passion to learn everything you possibly can about the investment banking business, then you are a top candidate for an investment banking internship.

Tips For Preparing For An Investment Banking Internship

Preparing for a banking internship is extremely important. This will be an **80 to 90 hour** a week adventure.

Since you already got the job, you've probably studied terms and scenarios in the business. **You should continue to study whenever you have time.** This is a learning process that doesn't end once you're hired. Continue to read the top ranked publications on investing and investment banking. You can never be too knowledgeable. Read about current events within the investment banking community. Stay current on deals within the industry.

Hyperink Note: Investment Banking publications include US Banker, The Banker and Banking Technology. Stay current with the Wall Street Journal and Economist.

Get into the mindset that you'll work **14 to 16 hours a day**; that is likely to be the case. You need to keep yourself in pretty good shape because you will be working most of the hours you are awake during the week.

You should try to set up a healthy eating plan so that you can stay alert and focused. Don't eat junk food because you may not be able to work as long eating an unhealthy diet.

Work in 30 minutes or an hour a day when you can take a run or do yoga or some sort of exercise. When you get back to your desk from your workout you will be refreshed and able to continue your work with more vigor. Exercise will reduce your level of tension and stress. If you don't have a way of doing this it may cause you to become slower and less focused because you have no way to get the stress released in your body and mind.

Go out on Friday and Saturday nights to blow off steam. This is very important because on Monday morning, you will be ready to go again in a big way. If you don't get away from work and have some fun and think about other things, you will get burnt out and you won't be able to do as good a job as if you weren't burnt out.

Have a high degree of attention and focus during your work time. That is why it is important to eat well and give yourself time during each day and on the weekends to relieve the stress from your mind and body so that you can continue to work at your highest level.

Hyperink Takeaway: Read publications to know current events and deals. Keep focused and efficient by eating well, exercising and enjoying weekends.

4 Tips For Getting An Internship If You're Not At A Top School

Many companies like to hire their interns from top schools,but if you're not at a top school, you can still get an internship.

Use the same networking strategies as the top contenders:

1. **Network effectively.** Get out of your comfort zone and go to financial events. Attend public meetings held by investment banks. Show interest in the subject while you are there. Introduce yourself.
2. If your school holds networking events, go and **introduce yourself** to the bankers.
3. Find out if you can attend **events held by other schools**. Network while you're there.
4. Find **alumni** from your own school at investment banks. Send them your resume and a letter. Don't forget a stock pitch.

The main thing to remember during the whole process don't give up. **Showing the drive to get what you want will come through.** Your personality and perseverance will be noticed, even if you are not from a top school.

Don't let details get in the way of what you want. Your passion for the business is much more important than the school you attend, so stay the course.

Remember Boutique Firms: 4 Tips For Securing A Position At A Boutique Firm

Most people looking for a summer internship look at the major brand name companies for their positions. While most of the big-name companies look for juniors for their internships, if you're a freshman or a sophomore, you shouldn't forget to look at the smaller, boutique firms for internships. Even if you're a junior or senior and find that you can't get a position with a large bank, **consider boutique firms. You will get similar experience and you may be exposed to a lot more things than at a larger company.**

There are hundreds of small, **boutique-type firms** in major metropolitan areas like New York, San Francisco, Los Angeles, and Chicago. These firms will hire freshman and sophomores as well as juniors.

4 Tips For Securing A Position At A Boutique Firm:

1. **The best way to get a position with these firms is to "spam" them. Send them your resume and cover letter along with a stock pitch. Send these to 100 firms or 200 firms.** You may get 10 responses to your email marketing scheme. If you get one or two interviews, you should get hired by one of them. This is a great way to get experience early if you think this is the career path you are going to take.
2. **Use your alumni directory.** Send your resume and other material to companies that have hired people from your school. Alumni may hire interns. Every connection you can make is important. **Networking** is the name of the game for getting into this industry.
3. **Expand your horizons.** Send your resume and accompanying documents to **mutual fund companies, hedge funds**, and other types of investment companies. Competition is pretty fierce, so don't leave any stone unturned. You want to get your name out there and make sure that every person who can hire you sees your name.
4. **Don't give up.** If you keep fighting to gain an internship, you'll succeed. If you're in your freshman or sophomore years, working for the summer at a boutique firm will be more valuable than just taking extra classes in the summer, so go for it!

Networking

"Researching the firm and coming prepared with□
questions is the 20% of the work that will drive 80% of
your networking results."

Have Fun Networking

When you talk to bankers, do you start off with business questions? Are you "all business, all the time"?

I used to do this things got boringquickly. Then, one day I was having a conversation with a mentor of mine at Goldman and he said, "You know Erin, you're really good at cutting through all the bullshit and getting straight to the point. You're almost too good!"

And I realized–I had forgotten to ask him how he was doing, how his day was, and if he had plans for the weekend!

So right after he said that I back-tracked and said, "John, oh my goodness, how are you doing? How was your day? Any plans for the weekend?"

He laughed and replied, "You're a fast learner!"

Going forward, I learned to make the "how are you doing" part of my business phone conversations the best and most exciting part.

Look at the **difference between the 2 conversations**, starting with the **all business** call and ending with a more personalized chat:

Erin: Hi John, thanks so much for taking my call!

John: No problem, just got off a deal so good timing! *tired voice*

Erin: Great! Can you tell me about why you think the Google / Groupon deal fell apart and how I should answer that question if someone asked me that in an interview?

John: Yeah, sure, so let's see….*business mode*

Instead, **personalize your conversation**:

Erin: John! Good morning!

John: Hey Erin, how are you?

Erin: Doing well! Thanks so much for taking my call, I really appreciate you making the time!

John: Yeah, no problem.

Erin: Do you have any exciting plans for this weekend? I'm so glad its Friday!

John: Haha yeah *internally thinking TGIF.* Well, I was going to head out tonight with some buddies from college so it should be good.

Erin: Oh nice! Are they your good friends?

John: Yeah, we're pretty good friends, we play soccer together on the weekends.

Erin: That's awesome. I played soccer the other day actually!

John: Oh yeah? *perks interest* Do you play a lot?

Erin: I wish! It was so much fun, we had soccer, beer, and great music in the park. It was a fantastic day.

John: *relaxed and now in fun-mode* Yeah tell me about it. Do you have any exciting plans this weekend?

So you see, lengthening the "how are you" can really turn into a full-fledged "let's find common interests and bond together" fun conversation if you ask the person about his or her plans. You can facilitate this by **researching the person** as much as possible on Facebook or LinkedIn and trying to find commonalities that you can bring up in conversation.

Some great starting points for me are Texas, running and sports, going out drinking, and food. The longer I draw out the introductory part, the more I feel like I'm friends with the person the next time I talk to them on the phone. It makes such a big difference.

You almost want them to go "oh no, we only have 10 minutes left, quick, ask me your questions before I jump in on my conference call" and then they'll want to talk to you next time around because you were so much fun the first time.

Lengthening that first part of the conversation is my first strategy This works best over the phone or in a 1:1 setting and not so much at an info-session where people mainly expect you to ask more formal questions. Not every banker I called was receptive to this. Some of them were on a really tight time crunch and you just have to respect that.

If you can't talk on the phone, send an email. If a banker doesn't respond to an email in a day – they're swamped. If they don't respond to you in 2+ days, send them a second email. *If they don't respond to that second email, then move on.*

It helps to keep your email very short and to the point. I'm talking **5 sentences max**. Bankers are more likely to respond to shorter emails because it's easier.

Becoming A Super Star Intern Isn't Only About Hard Work

A lot of interns, when they're starting out at an investment bank, **will get too caught up in their work**. Like me when I first started, they'll spend all of their time sitting at their desk and working every minute.

Networking, however, is the thing that will ultimately make all of your hard work pay off.

3 Ways To Become A Super Star Intern:

1. **Pay attention to building relationships.** You should get up and talk to as many people as you can at the bank and build a network that will benefit you in the future. Even if you leave, sign an offer, and go somewhere else, having a wide array of contacts can really help your career. **The way people move up in corporations is by knowing the people who'll bring them up to the next level.**
2. **Know names.** The simple act of meeting people and having them know you on a **first name basis** is extremely important. I cannot emphasize that enough. You want to be the intern who is able to walk down the floor and know everybody on a first name basis. That's what it means to be a super star intern.
3. **Maintain your reputation for great work.** In addition to being excellent at networking, you must of course also strive for having **A+ level work** that's perfect all of the time. No one is going to want to go out of their way to hire or work with you if they know that your work is sloppy and your work ethic is lacking.

Building A Network With The People In Your Intern Class

When you get accepted into an internship program at a major bank like JPMorgan, you'll be a part of a large group of other freshly arrived interns attending basic training with you. For my intern class, **I was in a group of around 150 people all in the same room for training.**

Your intern class is the easiest group to network with. You'll see each other a lot during the 1st week of the internship, which is a great time to start getting to know people.

All you have to do is go up to someone and say, "Hey, we're in the same intern class!" And from there it's **automatic bonding.** You'll learn things about each other like where you came from and what you like to do for fun, and you'll start meeting each other's friends.

A lot of the interns in the same division all hang out together. It's really easy because the people in your intern class will be very similar to you. **A lot of them will be college kids with similar interests who like going out and having a drink.**

In terms of having fun and building friendships, there's no better group than your intern class.

Investment Banking Mentors: How To Find And Learn From A Mentor

If you really want to learn the ins and outs of your trade, you'll need a lot of guidance from a mentor. Sometimes investment banks will give you a mentor. Other times you'll have to find your own. Either way, **it is always possible to create lasting relationships with people who can teach you a lot about your trade.**

Finding Your Own Mentor in a Mentorless Work Environment

1. **Create your own**. When I was working at FT, we had partners. There wasn't a formal mentor relationship structure. . I chose my mentor from the group of analysts working around me; anyone with a lot of experience on the job can be your mentor.

2. **Maintain a friendly relationship.** I decided that I would build a relationship with my chosen mentor by coming to his desk every morning and greeting him, which is something I did with my boss as well. **Little steps can set you apart and build a beneficial relationship with your mentors.** The mentor I chose just so happened to also be the person who gave me work, which was awesome. Sometimes you can find out a lot more about the basic structure of your work environment by getting to know the people above you.

3. **Ask for feedback.** Roughly once per week I would approach my mentor and ask for feedback. I'd say, "How am I doing?" Or, "I feel like I'm not doing so well with this. What do you think?" My interactions with my mentor were really just casual like that. You'll learn a lot from them and gain their respect by showing your eagerness to improve.

4. **Be casual, but professional.** When I first started approaching my mentor, I was really formal about it. I planned on establishing a formal relationship where we met, filled up papers, and critiqued each other. But that ended up being too lame, so I decided to go forward with a casual approach instead. When it comes to building close relationships in business, being casual and friendly, but still professional, is really the way to go.

Investment Banks With Formal Mentor Programs

At JPMorgan there was actually a formal mentor structure. They would assign you to experienced people based on your interests. They assigned me mentors from both inside and outside my division.

However, this formal mentor program wasn't nearly as beneficial or rewarding as my relationship with my personally chosen mentor. I only met with my assigned mentors once every three weeks, so they were really just check-in points to ensure that I was doing okay. They were also not from my specific group, so **they didn't have much of the detailed advice I wanted.**

3 Tips For Finding An Informal Mentor:

1. **Choose from within your working group.** Because I wasn't getting what I needed out of the formal mentor program, I had to choose my own mentor from within my working group. With my chosen mentor I was able to talk to them about my worries, my need for more work, or pretty much anything that I needed to talk about.

2. **Meet outside of work.** My relationship with my informal mentor was also friendly and casual. We met each other about once a week for dinner. Having that close relationship with someone from my own group was extremely helpful.

3. **Just ask**. If you're looking for a mentor, my advice is to just go out, find someone you think can teach you a lot, and **directly ask them if they're willing to guide you**. You'd be surprised how willing people are to help you when you demonstrate your willingness to improve yourself.

Unconventional Networking: Elevator Wait Times

One of the things you'll notice when you first work in offices at New York is the ridiculously long elevator times. **A lot of buildings have 80 to 100 floors for the elevator to go through,** so you end up spending 5 or more minutes per elevator trip just waiting there.

A lot of people spend elevator time just waiting quietly for their floor. I, however, was trying to become more proactive in terms of networking, so I decided that I wouldn't waste the time I spent in elevators.

Whether the other person in the elevator was a janitor or a vice chairman, I would make it a point to talk to them. I would turn to them, offer a handshake, and introduce myself, saying, "Hi, my name is Erin. I'm an intern here. Pleased to meet you."

Most of the people were initially surprised by my willingness to talk to everyone because they new that I was an intern, and most interns and regular employees don't take the time to go out and meet with people.

I felt that the simple act of talking to anyone on the elevator was a great networking hack because **before I knew it, I had a wide array of elevator friends in various divisions of the bank**, from many different floors. Being able to build and maintain a wide network is a very important part of investment banking, and I was able to do that just by taking advantage of otherwise wasted elevator time.

Not all people will work at tall buildings with lots of floors, especially a lot of people working in California. For them **an equivalent approach could be just saying hi to people in the hallway** and learning their names. Once you get in the habit of talking to people, you can even start having short conversations every day.

At the very least you should **learn the names of the people you bump into regularly**. If you're going to see these people every day, you might as well know their names, so you can say hi to them and eventually befriend them.

Jimmy Lee's To-Do List: A Crash Course In Networking

My biggest role model as an intern was Jimmy Lee. He is the current vice chairman of JPMorgan. He is one of a handful of people in line to be the CEO. **One of the things he invented was the syndicated loan,** which was the finance product I worked on in New York.

Jimmy Lee first inspired me when he gave a talk to the intern class I was in. His talk was loaded with a lot of information and advice that I really took to heart. I followed one particular piece of advice from him and had amazing results, so **I emailed him directly and told him that I'd followed his advice and succeeded.**

Jimmy Lee's Networking To-Do List

I also learned a lot about how to maintain several networking relationships by observing him. Every morning he writes down a list of the 50 clients he needs to talk to that day. This is basically his to-do list for the day because **at his level a lot of the important work revolves around relationship management and building trust with clients.**

During the beginning of my internship, I felt that I wasn't networking nearly as much as I should, so **I decided to implement my own mini version of Jimmy Lee's networking to-do list.** Every morning, I would write down a list of three people that I needed to contact that day, but when I actually started actively contacting people my list of three quickly ended up as a list of ten.

Through Jimmy Lee's example, I learned how important it is to consistently practice networking on a daily basis.

The Importance Of Networking While Interning

You won't succeed in the investment banking industry just by working well at your desk. No matter how good you are at crunching numbers and making charts, you cannot succeed without building a network.

At the beginning of my internship, I didn't realize this. Investment banking is more about people than it is about cents and dollars. If instead of sitting at your desk all day, you're making yourself visible and reaching out to people, you will build a lot of trust-based relationships in business. **Those relationships are what will get you deals in the future.**

Networking doesn't only have to be with clients and your co-workers. You can also build relationships with the people way high up in your organization if you're willing and confident enough to reach out to them.

For example, at JPMorgan, I ended up meeting with Jimmy Lee, who is one of the people at the very top of the JPMorgan hierarchy. If I hadn't actively gone out and asked to meet with Jimmy Lee, I wouldn't have had that opportunity.

In a company like JPMorgan that promotes actively meeting with senior managers, **the interns that boldly go and actually meet with senior management people are more likely to be on the radar of their superiors.** This can lead to more opportunities in the future that interns who were too scared to meet with senior managers will miss out on.

20 Solid Questions To Ask At Info Sessions

Let's say you're doing your homework in advance of an upcoming info session, and you get stuck trying to figure out what super amazing and insightful questions to ask the investment bankers. Luckily, you really don't need genius-questions, you just need **solid questions**.

I categorized some general questions into **4 groups below**, feel free to use them at your info sessions.

1. Learn about the analyst.

- How did you choose investment banking / sales and trading / capital markets?
- What's your favorite part of the job?
- Are there any exciting deals that you've been working on lately?
- Could you elaborate on a day in your life at the office?
- Any advice for how I can be a strong candidate this year?

2. Learn about the company.

- How is the company organized / what are the main coverage and product divisions?
- How is the mergers and acquisitions group / consumer retail group / your group of interest organized?
- Aside from a summer internship, are there other programs that the company hosts like case study competitions or diversity programs?
- How large is a typical deal team and how does the work typically get split up?
- Where do analysts tend to go after their two years? Business school? Private equity?

3. Learn about the internship.

- What would a typical intern get to learn and do in the sales division?
- What would a typical intern get to learn and do in the investment banking division?
- What would a typical intern get to learn and do in the research division?
- Is there anything an outstanding intern has done that has impressed you that I can learn from?
- What type of training will we have? Will we still engage in training during the internship?
- What do interns typically get graded on during a performance review?
- What is your offer rate? Your accept rate?

4. Most importantly, get the business card.

- Thanks so much Janet! May I please have your business card? I'd love to stay in touch.
- It was such a pleasure meeting you, Tim, might I have your business card?

- It was great talking to you Steve! I have more questions – do you think I could call or email you sometime?

Once you get his or her business card, send out an email asking for a call. During the phone call you can then ask more personalized questions, for guidance and mentorship, and truly learn about the culture of the firm.☐

3 Steps To Winning Contacts At Info Sessions

Info sessions are the perfect occasion for you to be a networking ninja. They are one of the best ways to learn about investment banking by actually talking to the people who work there. The problem is, **many students mistakenly think they're all about the info relayed** to you during the first 30 minutes: the speech, the video, and the panel. Wrong! **Info sessions are all about – you guessed it– the networking**. You have to ninja your way in there and make things happen.

You can take the student approach and sit back in your chair, watch the presentation, and leave thinking you now know everything about Goldman Sachs. But does this guarantee your resume being placed in the interview pile? What differentiates the average attendee from the student who knows how to work the room? One word: **strategy**. So what's your info session strategy?

My info session strategy was to **meet analysts and associates who were receptive** to me, get their business card, and then email them ASAP to establish a mentor-based relationship. That mentor-based relationship would be my ticket into the interview room.

Let me teach you how you can do the same:

Pre-Info Session

Before walking into the session, it's important to

- wear a full suit
- research the firm beforehand
- come prepared with questions

Researching the firm and coming prepared with questions is the 20% of the work that will drive 80% of your networking results. You need to have some kind of material from which to springboard into conversations, right?

Step 1: Meet bankers who are receptive to you.

The moment you walk into the room, turn on your aggressive networking self and start introducing yourself to people. Early in the show the bankers will most likely be standing in the back of the room together waiting for the brave college student to initiate contact– **walk up to them, shake their hand, and start talking**.

While you're listening to the info session speakers, choose who you want to network with and start thinking of questions you can ask. Once the presentation is over, be the first to walk up to your targeted bankers, shake their hand, introduce yourself, and ask your questions. You have do this fast or else you'll be squeezing into a circle. Be friendly, upbeat, energetic. Start off with, "How was your flight?" or "I really liked your advice about XYZ! Do you think I could try ABC?" That'll get the conversation going in a warm direction and it'll become more of a conversation and less of a dry, boring Q&A about banking.

Step 2: Get the business card!

While you're having this conversation, people will start trickling in and even interrupting and asking questions of their own. **Resist the urge to punch them in the face**. Instead, focus your energy on making your exit and getting the business card before you leave. After 1-2 interruptions say something like, "Hey John, it was such a pleasure meeting you!" Before Sarah asks another question– "Might I have your business card? I'd like to stay in touch."

And that's it! Take their card and find another person to meet. You may have to break into a new circle, but the moment you step in (let the banker finish what he's saying) shake his hand, introduce yourself, and ask a question. Keep your introduction short, just state your first name, grade, and major. Ask the next banker a couple questions and **when you're ready, get the business card and bounce**.

With my experience I've found it takes about **an hour to do this with 2-3 bankers** at a typical info session. Focus on quality of potential relationships not quantity of business cards. It's not about who walks out with the most business cards, **it's about developing a relationship** with someone you want to work with and who wants to work with you! And if that someone becomes your mentor, that's cherry on the cake.

Step 3: Email them after the session and establish a mentor-based relationship.

When you get home, send them an email that same night, no more than 3 sentences. Thank them and ask for a phone call or offer to treat them out to coffee. If you noticed something unique about them – for example – if they share your expertise in tequila or if their late-night snack of choice is chocolate chip cookies – maybe schedule a tequila tasting session or go for a gourmet cookie run.

You'll want to start a mentor-based relationship to

1. ask them all your questions about the bank and the group
2. ask them how you can best prepare yourself for the bank's recruiting season
3. get to know them better

This is the best way to **do your due-diligence**. Aim to strengthen and build relationships over time so that by the time you have to submit your resume, you have a solid strategy, a prepared resume, and you can call up your mentor to make sure you get the interview. With your mentor on your side, you're so much more likely to get an interview than someone who simply submitted his resume online.

Extra Tips for the Info Session Super-Networking-Ninjas:

- You might want to **take notes** so consider bringing a small note pad. Don't laugh: writing down someone's interests (hometown, favorite sports team, favorite drink, weekend hobby) and using that topic to start a future email is a way better than forgetting because you didn't write it down!
- **Come 15 minutes early** to survey the room, get in the zone, and score extra quality networking time.
- **Network with HR** and find an HR partner. It may not be apparent how having an HR partner is beneficial to you right now but later in the internship it'll be incredibly helpful to have people supporting you and your career in every division and at every level of the company.

How To Email An Investment Banker: Templates

You just came from an info session and, after much hard work, hold in your hands a very prized business card. Now you have to write an email asking for a call and to stay in touch.

What do you write?

I recommend keeping your email short and respectful. Aim for a 3-5 sentences.

I wrote up **2 simple email templates** below, just for you. Use and customize them!

Email to a Senior Banker

Dear Mr. Walter,

It was a pleasure meeting you at the info session this evening. I was the psychology student who asked you about balancing running marathons and banking. I really liked your talk about the Tesla IPO and I'd love to learn more from you about life and careers. Might I be able to call you sometime this week?

Sincerely,

Erin

It's unlikely that you're actually going to get this call. Most senior bankers simply don't have time. But you should still reach out and keep in touch with them. I send occasional emails and keep my senior bankers **updated on my recent accomplishments**. Even though I'm currently too inexperienced to be worth his or her time, who knows what opportunities may lie in the future?

Email to an Analyst or Associate

Hi Sarah,

It was great meeting you at the info session today. I was the student with whom you discussed parasailing. I had such a great time meeting you and I'm really excited about the Financial Sponsors group. May I call you to learn more about how I can prepare myself for this wonderful opportunity?

All the best,

Erin

You're much more likely to get a response and call from an analyst or associate. If you can **tie in a fun non-work-related topic** (like parasailing), brownie points for you!

Investment Banking Networking Bootcamp

Networking. Ah, what a word.

When I started college I didn't view networking in the most positive light. I didn't understand it. It seemed it was all about artificially chit-chatting at conferences to find people to further your career.

A couple books and major paradigm shifts changed that. I'd say *How to Win Friends and Influence People* by Dale Carnegie was the most earth-shattering of them all. *Never Eat Alone* by Keith Ferrazzi sparked my desire to leap out of my comfort zone and talk to people.

Networking is a skill just like math and public speaking. You get better at it the more you work at it and the better you get at it, the more possibilities you create in life. It takes breaking out of comfort zones to get better at it, but when you finally do, you realize it's not that bad, that it's actually quite fun, and that you're actually very good at it. You'll wonder why you made such a fuss about it in the first place. And just like math and public speaking, I find that networking isn't just applicable to business, its practicality as a skill transcends those boundaries and enables you to find and connect with simply interesting people. So if you choose to learn it, don't just learn it for breaking into banking, learn it for the rest of your life.

3 Steps To Winning At J.P. Morgan Winning Women

Congratulations! You've Got A Ticket To NYC And A Chance To Network With Some Of J.P. Morgan's Top Female

Bankers. Awesome.

The format of the J.P. Morgan Winning Women program may change every year, but it's possible to network and get a job offer by attending the event and impressing the people you meet. Even though I didn't attend Winning Women, I know a couple of rockstar girls who went and got summer internship offers shortly after.

Here is how you can do the same:

Step 1: Dress to Impress and Bring Your Best Handshake

Don't let the relaxed atmosphere fool you. It's an informal group interview. You're all being evaluated as potential summer analysts and you've got to **come prepared to impress**. You've got to **look sharp and be sharp**.

Wearing a **well-fitted full suit** is only the beginning. Investing in a solid suit, one that makes people go, "Wow, you look great!" can do a lot for your professional polish. Does your suit have the "you look great" factor? Test it– walk around and ask your dorm mates for feedback. Don't skimp on your suit. Invest. Black is the most formal color but you can also go with a dark gray. I'd stick to white or light blue blouses. Good suits should look like Theory Suits, so study the look.

You also want to **bring dressy attire** in case there's a dinner social. I'm talking dressy skirt and dressy blouse. Or a shapely and modest dress in a dark color with a suit jacket. You're safest if you stick to knee-length skirt, but it's totally fine to go sleeveless and show off your arms. Why the dress? Why can't you just wear your suit? Well, you can go with a suit. But in a business social event, **wearing stylish, classy, and dressy attire can give you a distinct networking advantage**. In business social events, people want to relax and have a good time with their work colleagues. If you go in your suit, you're implicitly advertising that you're in **work mode**.

But if you dress up a bit, you're advertising "Hey, I'm a banker and I know how to have fun." The "I know how to have fun" factor will draw people to you. After all, we naturally gravitate to people who we can have a good time with. *Dressing up facilitates this gravitation*. I can almost assure you that you're going to have an easier time networking when you attend a business-social event in social attire. Check out Banana Republic dresses to get an idea.

For the formal part of the event, **bring a notebook and your resume**. Take notes at presentations so that you can actually *take home what you've learned* about the firm. Also write down interesting facts about some of the people that you meet so that you can bond after the event. For example, if you learn that Sarah really likes formula-drift, when you write a follow-up email to stay in touch with her you can creatively add a *P.S. I'm excited for the formula-D final rounds in Malaysia this summer! Wouldn't it be awesome to steal away to a vacation there and get to watch the championships?* **Adding that personal touch** will enable you to stand out and also show off your multi-faceted personality.

In your notebook, come prepared with questions to ask bankers. Do some due diligence before the event and write down 5-10 things you'll want to ask. If you're not sure what to ask, check out *How to Ask Solid Questions At Info Sessions* on this site. You don't just want to write questions to **impress people** because questions typically don't, but you want to come prepared to soak up as much as possible and having questions will help you do that more effectively.

Last and definitely not least, **bring your resume!** Even though there will be a resume workshop session, don't bring in a crappy resume! Instead, **come in with a super polished and super awesome resume**, one that's dramatically different and better from the one you sent in with your application. Before you go, have at least 5 people with previous investment banking experience give feedback. If only a couple people have looked at it, it's probably not good enough. You'll be surprised how coming there with a super-polished resume will set you apart from the other girls. You'll want your resume to be so polished that the senior banker reviewing it will keep it and tell HR, "We need to hire her!"

Recap list of things to bring:

- Full suit
- Dressy attire for evening dinner event
- Notebook
- Questions to ask bankers
- Resume

Step 2: Network Like a Rockstar

If you haven't networked before, visit my Networking Bootcamp section and read all the articles. Don't be a wallflower, be a networking rockstar. Instead of shyly talking to other girls from your school who you already know, venture out of your comfort zone and talk to full-time employees whenever you have a chance. I recommend talking with analysts first and warming up before talking to senior bankers. Just to recap seniority from least to most experienced:

Analyst (Most Junior Person)
Associate
VP
MD
Vice Chairman
Executive (Most Senior Person)

Start with analysts and associates and get in the groove before you network with VPs and MDs. When you're talking to them, start off with a firm handshake and a strong introduction. "Hi I'm Erin Parker *handshake* very pleased to meet you!" After you ask them your questions and listen to their stories, **ask for their business card**. *"Sarah I'd really love to stay in touch— may I please have your business card?"* You have to get these business cards! **You can't expect them to remember you, because they won't!** So ask for their business card so you can get in touch with them after the event.

Don't be shy. Make the ask.

Step 3: Follow Up

Consider your networking efforts successful if you have **at least 3 business cards**. Ideally, you should have **5 or more.** On the airplane ride back, start drafting follow-up emails to all of these bankers. Feel free to use the template in How to Email Investment Bankers on this site. Keep your email to **3 sentences** and **make sure you attach your resume**. Yes, attach your resume. Why? So that they can easily forward the email to the person in charge of hiring and say, "I really liked this girl! Let's take her."

Now, make sure you include an **action item** in your follow up email.

An invitation to action or "action item" ensures that you keep in touch with the person after the event. A simple "Thank You" email has its limitations because it doesn't ask the banker to respond. An action item does.

Example Action Items

I would love it if you would please be so kind as to review my resume and let me know how I can make it better.

Would you be available for a quick call later this week? I'd love to talk to you and learn more about leveraged finance. ☐

It was great meeting you at the event: may I please meet you for coffee this week to learn how I can best prepare myself for the summer internship?

See? Calls to action very clearly invite future interaction. Now that's powerful.

And of course, if you have a special bonding point, include that in the email as well. It can be anything from formula-D to macadamia nut cookies to vacations in the Caribbean. It's like the cherry on top!

Recap of what to include in your follow-up email:

- Resume
- Invitation to Action
- Special bonding point

Now that you know what to do, put everything else aside and start preparing!

I wish you the best of luck and hope that offer comes to your inbox.

As always, feel free to contact me at breakintobanking [at] gmail [dot] com with any questions!

5 Steps To Mentorship-Based Investment Banking Networking

A critical (read: *absolutely critical, not optional*) part of the recruiting process is **networking**. The financial crisis has changed the way recruiting markets operate. You have to be a lot more strategic, aggressive, and prepared. Investment banking networking is a completely different beast. It's okay though: you have me as your guide. You'll be fine!

Step 1: Write a list of all the places where you want to work.

Write a list of all the companies and groups you want to explore. Be specific. For example, your top 3 choices may be J.P. Morgan Financial Institutions Group, Goldman Sachs Technology, Media, Telecom Group, and Morgan Stanley Financial Sponsors. Next to each group, write down the names of analysts and associates you know, or a list of people who could introduce you to analysts and associates in your groups. **Make your list detailed and extensive**, it will serve as the foundation of your investment banking network.

Step 2: Tap your current network to build your investment banking network.

Send an email to the analysts and associates on your list and **ask for a phone call**. If you don't know anyone in your desired groups, ask friends, family members, professors, or mentors for introductions. Keep your email **3-5 sentences** and attach your resume.

Step 3: Call and find mentors to guide you through recruiting.

Start calling! Every call is an opportunity to learn about the group and impress your contact. **What starts as a phone call can become a solid mentorship.** Investment banking networking goes beyond surface-level schmoozing; I believe it's about building mentorships and finding people who can guide you and help you. Ask for advice and keep in touch with the person so that he or she can show you the ropes throughout recruiting. As recruiting approaches, you should **call several people a week.** I know you have classes and student groups and other commitments, but you have to make the time to network and be mentored because it's critical to getting the interview. It's way more important to build these relationships and get a job than it is to study for one of your classes and not have a job! **It's better to have a 3.5 GPA and a job offer than a 4.0 GPA and be unemployed.**

So how do you handle these calls? What's the best way to do it?

Treat your contacts like you would treat a friend–ask them how they're doing, smile while you're talking, make it an enjoyable experience. Your goal, by the end of the call, is to be buddies. Investment banking networking isn't all about business, it's all about **building these relationships**.

Tell them you'd like to learn about the group and **ask questions**! Ask them for **feedback** on your resume, your cover letter, and your candidacy. Ask them what the upcoming interview process is going to look like, how you can best prepare for it, and how you can improve.

Step 4: Use your new contacts to deepen your network.

Now here's the key: **ask your current contact for another contact at the same bank**. For every person you network with, ask for one more contact. If someone asks you, "So you want to work for JP Morgan? Who do you know there?" You want to answer, "I know 3 people in the Financial Institutions Group, 3 people in Debt Capital Markets, 2 people in Syndicated & Leveraged Finance, and 4 in Financial Sponsors! And they're all my super-awesome mentors." Compare that type of response to, "Oh um, well I met someone at an info session once, I think his name was John?" You want to grow and deepen your network. **So every time you meet someone new, ask them to introduce you to someone else!** If the banker likes you, they'll want to introduce you to 10 other people in the group so feel free to ask them for more contacts. Investment banking networking revolves around this. The point is, make the ask.

Step 5: Close the deal– ask for the interview and follow up with next steps.

Be aggressive with your networking and have a sense of urgency. Stay in touch with your mentors throughout your recruiting cycle and keep iterating your story and your resume to make sure you get the interview. If you're unsure as to whether you're going to get the interview: ask! Say something like, "Dave I really want to thank you for your mentorship so far, I just want to make sure I'm on track to get an interview. If I am, what should I be preparing for? If not, is there anything more I can do to ensure that I'm a competitive candidate?" When it's time to turn in your resume, send each of your mentors a **personal email thanking him or her** for the help and let him or her know that you turned in your (attached) resume to HR. This ensures that your mentors have your resume, HR has your resume, and that you're in the running!

Tips For Smart Networking For Your IBanking Internship

Networking is the best way to get an investment internship; however, networking properly is very important.

At information forums and alumni networking events in the banking industry, show respect to the bankers attending. Go to these meetings with the right mindset. You are there to help yourself get into the business, but that should not be blatant. The bankers know why you are there; you don't have to be overbearing. **If you are truly passionate about the industry, this will show in your personality and interest in the subject.**

Introduce yourself to the bankers at the event and express your **sincere interest**. Don't try to fake an interest. If you're not sure you want to go this route, you won't be taken seriously. **Decide** if this is what you want and, if it is, get into it.

When you are attending functions where bankers are speaking, **ask questions** like, "What made you decide to get into this business?" or "What is it like to work in the investment business?" People like to tell stories about how they got started and what led them in the direction they took.

Ask them for their **business card.** You will have their direct email address so you can send them a **follow-up email.** Don't hand them your business card. Remember in these get-togethers **what you can do for them should be the primary focus,** not what they can do to help you further your goals. Don't make it seem like you are using them, even if this is the case; keep a curious and helpful mindset.

After attending these sessions, make sure to follow up with your resume and other pertinent information.

Recruiting

"Attend information forums put on by your school. You can learn a lot about the industry as well as meet some of the people from the major investment banks."

Banking Internship Programs: 3 Ways To Find And Win Internships

The Internet: Your First Research Tool

Even if you have a ridiculously strong resume, you'll need to locate internships before you do anything else.

The first place you should start during an internship search is the internet You should think about what banks where you'd like to get an internship and look them up on the internet.

I began my search just by **googling different listings of top banks on the internet and choosing where I should apply based partly on that.** The lists have probably changed because of the recession, but you should be able to finding these bank listings through a simple search.

After you have a list of banks you want to internship for, you can go straight to **each bank's website** and look around for internship information, but it can end up taking a lot of time going through all the different websites.

Using Your Career Center

Instead of looking at bank websites to find out which ones offer internships, I went to my school's **career center**, made an Excel spreadsheet, looked around at the **internship listings** they compiled, and wrote down any internships that applied to my goals and interests.

On the other hand, if it's past recruiting season for whatever bank you want to apply to, you can Google them, look up their contact information, and **cold call or email them**. Either way, using your career center will make the entire process so much easier.

The internet is a great tool for **finding out about the reputations** of different banks, but when it comes to **locating internship opportunities**, you should really take advantage of what your career center has to offer.

Diversity Programs

You can also take advantage of great internship opportunities by looking up the different **diversity programs** that each bank offers. Some of the interns that I met at JPMorgan applied through a diversity program.

Diversity programs help people with diverse background break into different career fields. **A lot of these programs also come with scholarships** to help pay for schooling.

One great program to check out is **Sponsors for Educational Opportunity** (SEO), which is a mentoring program that helps connect young job seekers from under-served areas with excellent work opportunities. There are also programs geared towards helping people with an **LGBT** background get into internships.

If you're willing to look around, there are lots of bank-specific programs for people from different backgrounds, but you'll have to spend some time researching the offerings of different banks to find these.

If, however, you aren't a diversity student and don't have an Ivy League background, you should keep an eye out for informational sessions and **make your presence known** there.

Banking Internship Applications: Staying Competitive After A Rejection

If you don't get accepted into any of your first choice internship programs, you'll always have the opportunity to **try again next year**. However, you will have to be careful about what you do between now and then, to **ensure that you're as competitive a candidate as possible** when your next chance comes around.

Your best bet in terms of boosting your desirability as an internship candidate is to **work at something closely related to the field you're trying to enter** That way, you'll be showing investment banks that you have the experience necessary to succeed. You'll also have the opportunity to sharpen and acquire new skill sets.

There's lots of different work opportunities that will increase your desirability as an intern. You could start working at an **investment management firm, a hedge fund, a venture capital firm,** and anything else that includes hands on work with different aspects of investment and finance. There are lots of alternatives to investment banking internships.

4 Suggestions For Effective Networking

Are you interested in getting an investment banking internship? It isn't as easy as it seems.

Many young people feel that all they have to do to get with a top name investment banking firm is to have a high GPA and be from a great school. That's not all that is required.

As a matter of fact, those traits may be helpful, but they are not the most important things to consider. Having a high GPA certainly helps, but you don't need to be from a top school to participate in an internship program. The most important thing now is to begin **networking** to meet people in the industry.

4 Suggestions For Effective Networking:

1. Attend **information forums** put on by your school. You can learn a lot about the industry and meet people from the major investment banks. Don't be afraid to go up and introduce yourself.
2. Go to **alumni functions** where there will be speakers from the investment banking community. Again, introduce yourself after the event. **Ask them for a business card.**
3. Attend other functions where there will be investment bankers. Getting in front of these people in a **face-to-face setting** is crucial.
4. After introducing yourself and expressing your interest in the industry, send a **follow-up email** with your resume, a cover letter and a stock pitch.

A lot of people feel that if you send enough resumes and emails alone, the numbers will work; someone will call you because you have such great credentials.

It just doesn't work that way anymore. There are tons of smart people who are vying for those same internships.

Investment banks get many of these emails and resumes every day. Why would yours stick out? **It might stick out because you put forth the effort to get out and meet some of these people face-to-face and introduce yourself.**

If you have gone to a function and talked with the bankers, sent your material and you don't hear back, don't give up. **Send the material again.** Maybe the person was too busy the first time around. After you send the material a second time, call and ask for an interview. The person will be more inclined to give you the interview because they know you. You stopped and talked to them at a previous event.

When you finally do get an interview, study for it. Be prepared with all the financial information that they could possibly throw at you. Make flash cards with the financial questions on one side and the answers on the other. Learn the answers until you can recite them in your sleep. Be personal and show an interest in your interviews– you should get a spot.

Resumes

"It's more impressive to see that you completed a part-
time internship doing M&A advisory at a boutique than it
is to see that you're involved in 27 student groups."

4 Investment Banking Resume Secrets

Here are 4 critical tweaks you can use to improve your investment banking resume:

#1. Internship Experience Is More Important Than Leadership In Student Groups

People often say, "I want to get an investment banking internship, but first I'll raise my GPA, become president of the finance group, volunteer on the side and then get an internship." Sounds like a very inefficient strategy, don't you think? If you want to get a banking internship, then *just get a banking internship*! I'm going to say it again: **if you want a banking internship, just get a banking internship!** It makes more sense to aim for a stint at a local boutique *right now* than to productively procrastinate by becoming president of your finance club before actually doing what it takes to get a job. Don't make any more creative excuses. Just do what it takes and get a job.

Another thing: **banks weigh work experience more heavily than your student group activities** because work experience more accurately illustrates the extent of your involvement in the industry. It's more impressive to see that you completed a part-time internship doing M&A advisory at a boutique than it is to see that you're involved in 27 student groups.

Now take a look at your investment banking resume. **What does your work experience consist of?** Is it heavy with student-group activities or real job experience?

#2. In your bullet points, focus on your deliverables as opposed to your responsibilities.

Responsibilities are nondescript, general tasks you were assigned. Deliverables are specific, tangible items that you completed. Take a look at the below examples.

Parker & Parker: Responsibilities Focus

- Responsible for staying on top of the markets via daily morning reports
- Assisted pitch book production in all the major deals across the company
- Completed weekly training assignments on DCF and Comps Model valuation methods

That sounds okay, right? Now watch this.

Parker & Parker : Deliverables Focus

- Crafted 50 healthcare and biotech market reports for senior management
- Produced 12 merger pitch books, 5 bridge loan presentations, and 3 amend and extend propositions
- Completed DCF model on Johnson & Johnson and a comps model on Bayer in firm-wide training program

I think you get the picture. This leads in to my 3rd point.

#3. Give numbers! Relay your results as quantitatively as possible.

Relaying your results in numbers is an incredibly effective way to show off your hard work.

Go through your investment banking resume and quantify your work, even your non-finance work.

For example, if you were in a non-profit, tell me *how much money you raised*, how big the audience was that you reached and what type of target-market analysis you completed. Same goes for volunteer work.

If you compete in a sport, tell me *what competitions you were in*, what medals you won and how many events you participated in.

If you do writing, music or film, tell me *how many books you sold*, how many views your videos receive, how many galleries your paintings are featured in.

If you have a website, tell me *how much traffic you get*, what your click-through rates are and what methods you use to monetize it.

If you started your own company, tell me your revenue, *how many customers you have*, how many products you've sold.

The best investment banking resumes are quantified. So give me the numbers!

#4. Write Interesting Interests.

In the bottom of your investment banking resume, have a line for your interests. I've read some of my friends' resumes and some of their interests were so impressively, cleverly worded (even though they were normal interests). Others just wrote their interests *normally* so it didn't stand out to me. If there's any line to be creative, this is the line to be a wordsmith.

Take a look at the below examples.

Normal Interests: coffee, running, mexican food, movies.

Interesting Interests: espresso-bar hopping, coastal marathons, burrito culinary techniques, 1980s sci-fi films.

The idea is to get into a *niche*. Take your general interest and ask yourself, "What is my niche?"

Now take a break from reading, whip out MS Word, and bank-ify your resume now. Utilize the tricks above and take your resume from *college* to banker in 30 minutes.

Structuring The Email Cover Letter

Say you're looking for a part-time stint at a boutique or middle market bank, that summer is coming near, and you don't have time to write a full cover letter. You need a job and you need something quick and dirty that you can send out to **hundreds of investment banks** to target the ones that are looking for your talent. This is where the **email cover letter** takes the stage.

Email cover letters need to be **short**, sweet, and to the point. Don't make them much longer than **3-5 sentences.** Let the bulk of your impressing documents be in an attachment. **Write the cover letter in such a way that they'll want to click on your resume** and learn more about you.

Here's an **example**:

Dear Dr. Kyle,

Please consider my attached resume and cover letter for an internship with East Advisors this summer. Because of my sophomore status I am willing to work unpaid or for university credit. I contend that I'm a strong candidate for your internship because of my strong financial background, quantitative skills, and previous finance work experience. I am ready to start as soon as possible, please feel free to email or call me at 123-456-7890.

I look forward to hearing from you soon.

Sincerely,

Erin Chan Parker

Other Sample Cover Letters:

- Sample Investment Banking Cover Letter – Personal Style
- Sample Investment Banking Cover Letter – Generic Style
- Sample Investment Banking Cover Letter – Email Style
- Write Investment Banking Cover Letters
- How To Transform Your Investment Banking Cover Letter From Generic To Personal

Writing Investment Banking Cover Letters

What's the deal with **investment banking cover letters**? Do bankers actually read them? Should you spend 20 hours writing yours?

Usually, **boutique firms** are more likely to read cover letters because they're smaller and care more about fit. Nevertheless, my cover letter was read everywhere I've interviewed and worked. *Somebody* reads them. **Make them work!** As for spending 20 hours writing them, well hopefully these articles can make that process much more **efficient**

The point of the cover letter is to **impress**. Impress them with your story, drive, interest in the company, and differentiating factors. Tell the bank why it should hire you and not the next guy.

Types of Cover Letters

There are three types of cover letters: the **personal cover letter**, the **generic cover letter**, and the **email cover letter**.

Sample Cover Letters:

- Sample Investment Banking Cover Letter – Personal Style
- Sample Investment Banking Cover Letter – Generic Style
- Sample Investment Banking Cover Letter – Email Style
- Write Investment Banking Cover Letters
- How To Transform Your Investment Banking Cover Letter From Generic To Personal

Structuring The Generic Cover Letter

A generic cover letter best accompanies an application to **a bank where you haven't quite gotten the chance to network** but where you think you have a serious shot at working at if your letter is good. This would work well for established boutiques who are recruiting at your school and looking at a small pool of applicants. **Start with a generic cover letter at the beginning of recruiting and personalize that letter after networking and meeting people.**

Again, the heading of your cover letter should match the heading of your resume. Your letter shouldn't exceed one page in length. Be sure to write to impress! Show off!

I recommend the following structure:

- **First Paragraph:** Introduce yourself. Talk about your **major and skills**. Include a **thesis** that lays out the structure of the remainder of your letter.
- **Second Paragraph:** Start impressing them early! You may not have the chance to write about people you've met so, **start off with a story about something awesome that you did**. Examples include leading a team and winning a competition for $25,000, managing your own stock portfolio and making $10,000 in profit, teaching yourself financial modeling before implementing a training program on campus. Impress them with your **accomplishments**, and if they're not "finance-related" then that's great, too! Remember that article I wrote about quantifying your resume? **Quantify your accomplishments** in your cover letter, too.
- **Third Paragraph:** Tie your skills and accomplishments into why you're pursuing finance and **why you're pursuing this internship**. People want to hire people with specialty, so what's your **specialty**? You do have a specialty. Don't be lazy, by basic comparative advantage economics you're going to be better at something than everyone else in the world. Figure out what that is and write about it. When you write your closing, **re-iterate your interest in the bank** and what you're looking to add to the team.

Here is an **example** of a generic cover letter:

Investment Banking Generic Cover Letter

Other Sample Cover Letters

- Sample Investment Banking Cover Letter – Personal Style
- Sample Investment Banking Cover Letter – Generic Style
- Sample Investment Banking Cover Letter – Email Style
- Write Investment Banking Cover Letters
- How To Transform Your Investment Banking Cover Letter From Generic To Personal

Structuring The Personal Cover Letter

In the personal cover letter, not only should you aim to impress them with your finance experience, knowledge, and drive, but you also want to go the extra step and write about the people in the team who you've met and how they've impacted your decision to apply. **The personal cover letter is personal because you include the people factor.**

The structure of the letter is important. First, the heading of your cover letter should match the heading of your resume. Your letter shouldn't exceed one page in length. That is a hard requirement.

How To Organize Your Cover Letter

First Paragraph: Introduce yourself. Talk about your major and skills. *Include a thesis* that lays out the structure of the remainder of your letter.

Second Paragraph: *Tell them your story.* Tell them why you're applying and why you're a great fit. Here is where you make it personal and mention all the names of people who you've spoken to, mentors you have at the bank, things you've learned from them, things you like about the group, and what you see yourself contributing.

Third Paragraph: Here is where you impress them with *your skills, your background, and your accomplishments.* Talk about the coolest things you've been working on. Tie that in to why you're pursuing finance and that particular internship. Close the letter by tying everything in to your thesis.

Here are 2 **examples** of my own cover letters for your reference:

Investment Banking Cover Letter Example #1

Investment Banking Cover Letter Example #2

A concise and well-constructed cover letter is your first step toward getting your dream internship.

Crafting The Personal Cover Letter

Writing a personal cover letter can be difficult. If you're applying to Goldman Sachs, a☐ personal cover letter needs to discuss in-depth why you'd like to work at Goldman Sachs and why you're the best candidate for the job. Most cover letters do a great job of relaying your strengths and previous accomplishments, but an employer must be convinced of **the "fit."**☐

In crafting a personal cover letter, there are **2 big questions** you need to ask yourself:

1. What are the three things that you can offer to Goldman Sachs that nobody else in the world can?

Every banker in the world is an ambitious type-A workaholic who gets shit done and makes a ton of money. You're not the only one! **What differentiates you?**

It took me awhile to think about my differentiating factors. I realized they don't have much to do with the analyst role. That's okay! Just make sure your differentiating factors are **real.**

As an example to guide your own answers, here's how I thought about **my differentiating factors:**

First of all, I love to lead. Second of all, I achieve every major goal I set. Third of all, I have amazing public speaking skills. So my differentiating qualities are that, "You're hiring a future leader of the company who will consistently achieve major milestones and have outstanding communication skills to guide the company forward."

What's your story? What makes you different from the other hard working, type-A personalities with outstanding recommendations and quantitative degrees with high GPAs?

2. When did you fall in love with Goldman Sachs? When was that moment?

When did your heart say, "Damn, Goldman Sachs is so freaking awesome! I want to work here forever!"

Find out when that moment happened. Ask yourself, "What do I love about this group?" Or, "What do I love about the people in this group?" There has to be a really **personal answer** to this because "I want to work for Goldman Sachs, because it's the best" is what everybody says.

Give it some thought to that moment. The answer isn't going to come fast. When it comes, it'll be great and genuine.

If you need some help figuring out what your greatest strengths are and what makes you☐ different from all the other type-A workaholics, **I highly recommend the following books** to help you craft your unique cover letter:

- Sample Investment Banking Cover Letter – Personal Style
- Sample Investment Banking Cover Letter – Generic Style
- Sample Investment Banking Cover Letter – Email Style

- Write Investment Banking Cover Letters
- How To Transform Your Investment Banking Cover Letter From Generic To Personal

Like What You're Reading? Spread The Word!

We're a small startup, so we rely on happy readers to help us grow (hopefully, that means you!).

Here are some specific ways you can contribute:

1. Share your success with us! Tell us how the book has helped you
2. Visit our website: www.ibankinginternship.com and comment on your favorite article
3. Ask our experts a question! We'll answer the best ones directly on the site
4. Like Us on Facebook
5. Send us your feedback or ideas at feedback@hyperinkpress.com!

To make it worth your time (and to thank you for bugging your friends / family), email us after you've done any of the above and we'll give you a **special bonus as thanks. Trust us, it's worth it!**

Thanks!

SAVE 40% ON ANY TITLE BELOW
WHEN YOU BUY NOW!

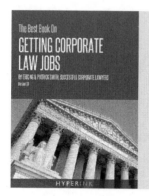

Printed in Great Britain
by Amazon.co.uk, Ltd.,
Marston Gate.